PILATES

The Essential Guide

Need
— 2 —
Know

Annabel
Kent

First published in Great Britain in 2010 by
Need2Know
Remus House
Coltsfoot Drive
Peterborough
PE2 9JX
Telephone 01733 898103
Fax 01733 313524
www.need2knowbooks.co.uk

Need2Know is an imprint of Forward Press Ltd.
www.forwardpress.co.uk
SB ISBN 978-1-86144-097-6
Cover photograph: istockphoto

Contents

Introduction

Pilates has grown and grown in popularity as a mind and body phenomenon. People everywhere are seeking ways to not only improve their physical health, but also to reduce stress levels in this fast paced world in which we live. This book will appeal to all those who are looking for a straightforward, user-friendly book about Pilates and want to improve both their health and wellbeing.

Pilates started as a celebrity trend and seemed only available to the very fit, but it has now become mainstream. Everyone is able to experience the many benefits Pilates has to offer. There is no age limit and it doesn't matter how fit you are. Pilates can help all individuals safely and effectively as it can be modified to suit all needs.

This book will enable you, the reader, to better understand the history and principles behind the movements. It is also an excellent introduction to those who are new to Pilates or who seek to deepen their knowledge. This book will not only help to prepare newcomers for classes, it will also teach you new ways of improving and getting the most out of a Pilates workout. This useful guide is not about sitting down and reading. It's about action. By arming you with the essentials, the exercises themselves will, through experiencing them, have you feeling and looking great.

This is a quick but valuable source of information about how to achieve all the benefits that this complete mind and body system has to offer. Pilates is a system of exercise that will enhance every aspect of your life and can be slotted into different lifestyles without any hassle.

Every chapter of the book is here for a concrete reason. All the foundations are clearly laid out for you to read and absorb so that you can progress in your workout and become more in control of your own body.

The exercises are explained in a friendly manner, as if an instructor is with you in the same room. The fundamentals provided before the main workout will produce a solid understanding for all the Pilates movements. They can then be applied to all the movements for you to get the most out of your session. You will soon find yourself walking down the street with improved grace and confidence.

I have provided modifications for you to start with and then progressions are offered with each exercise. At the end of this book you will find the advice and resources very useful should you want to find out more.

Disclaimer

Always consult your GP before changing your exercise regime if you have any medical condition. The author does not claim any medical qualifications and neither the author or the publishers will accept any liability for injuries resulting from or aggravated by the exercises contained within this book.

Chapter One

Welcome to Pilates

What is it?

Developed by a man called Joseph Pilates, this method of exercise is a total body programme that conditions both body and mind. It teaches you the correct mechanics of the human body and how to apply this to everyday life, which will keep you in the health that is normal and deserved.

The spine is very important in Pilates; according to Joseph himself, a poor state of spine health makes us feel old and tired. Therefore, Pilates works by targeting the deep postural muscles, bringing the body back into correct alignment so balance can be restored, thus changing the way you move and feel. It consists of a series of low repetition and low impact conditioning and stretching exercises that build core strength, using the principles of resistance. Pilates can be done on the mat or on the equipment devised by Joseph Pilates.

If there is stability and control in the torso then limbs can move freely without tension. Pilates is a series of controlled movements focusing on the torso that require a lot of concentration in order to perform them correctly; this in itself encourages the unison of both mind and body. The exercises tone and strengthen without adding muscle bulk, so you will find that you will walk with more grace and learn to use your body in the best way possible. Every muscle group is worked without mindless repetition of specific movements, which can cause over activity in some muscle groups and under activity in others. Therefore, Pilates provides a totally balanced workout, working on quality, not quantity.

'Pilates teaches you the correct mechanics of the human body and how to apply this to everyday life.'

Joseph Pilates brief biography

Joseph Hubertus Pilates was born in 1880 near Düsseldorf, Germany, and he lived to the age of 87. As a child he suffered from asthma, rickets and rheumatic fever. He was also bullied as a child and showed the strength of his character in his pursuit to not be a victim in life, but a survivor. To overcome his poor health, he became involved in a number of physical activities such as boxing, skiing, gymnastics and self-defence and he studied many self-improvement systems from both the east and the west. He was inspired by the ancient Greek ideal of a man perfected in body, mind and spirit. After being given an anatomy book, he learned every page and every detail of how the body works. By the time he was 14, he developed a strong, fit and healthy body to model for anatomy charts.

In 1912, Joseph moved to England where he became a boxer, circus performer and a self-defence instructor. But when the First World War broke out in 1914, he was put into internment camps. It was during this time that he taught physical training to the other inmates and he rehabilitated those who had been injured during the war.

In 1926, after the war, Joseph left for America. It was on the journey over there that he met his wife to be, Clara. Together they started a studio on Eighth Avenue in New York in the same building as several dance studios. Joseph was closely associated with dance, providing conditioning and rehab from injury and training of the dancers. He continued to develop and scientifically prove his own exercise training method for co-ordinated physical and mental health which he called 'Contrology'; this is now what we know today as 'Pilates'. Joseph may have been a health guru, but he was also known to be the life and soul of the party. He believed in fitness supporting life's richness.

The many benefits

- Correct posture and alignment.
- Body awareness.
- Enables optimal function of internal organs.
- Improves balance and co-ordination.

- Improves flexibility.
- Reduces stress levels.
- The focus on breathing will bring physical and psychological benefits.
- Enhances skills in other sports and daily activities.
- Promotes mind and body connection.
- Increases muscle tone and strength.
- Increases bone density.
- A flatter stomach and trimmer waist through focus on core muscle activation.
- Develops a strong, lean and supple body.

How to use this book

To get the most from the exercises provided in this book, it is important to understand the basic principles of Pilates, especially if you are a beginner. Take your time to understand and absorb all the information and fundamentals (the building blocks) before you rush into the main exercise programme. If you don't, you will miss the vital point of the method. It would be like building a house with bricks without first cementing them into place.

I would always strongly recommend that you have at least a few sessions with a Pilates teacher as over the years we all develop bad habits which may feel normal. A teacher will help you identify these and teach you how to correct them.

Everything in this book is set out in a purposeful order that will take you on a journey towards a healthy new you. After familiarising yourself with the basic information, principles and fundamentals, you will then be instructed to put the fundamentals into practice. After these are firmly in place (take your time!), you will then be able to apply the fundamentals to the main workout programme.

You have been given modifications, with the exercises becoming progressively harder. Only move on when you can perform the beginner movements correctly without strain. You can stay with the modifications permanently and still experience the many benefits as long as you are performing them correctly.

'To get the most from the exercises provided in this book, it is important to understand the basic principles of Pilates, especially if you are a beginner.'

In time, you will become familiar with the names of the exercises, allowing you to deepen your workout with more focus and intensity. You cannot be expected to perform the advanced versions of all the Pilates movements straightaway. Therefore, all the movements will be presented in three stages. Only move on to the next stage when you have practised the first stage correctly, incorporating all the Pilates principles and fundamentals at each stage. Moving on to the next level will depend on many factors such as how regularly you exercise and any present or previous injuries.

It is important to remember that we are not all built the same, so different movements will suit your body type more than other movements. Therefore, you must only work at your own level, keeping within your present range of movement. Remember, you are not in competition with anyone else. The main goal is to make improvements at your own pace; we are all individuals.

Every advanced movement in Pilates is built on the basics, and mastering the basics is essential to furthering work in Pilates. The challenge is to keep true to the quality of the work as the exercises become more complex. As you develop more awareness of your body, you will then learn to understand your range of movement at each stage. Try to take your time and be patient – your body deserves it.

Before you begin

- As with any exercise programme, it is recommended that you consult a healthcare professional before you begin.

- Create a safe environment to work in as you don't want to bang into furniture or walls.

- Try to avoid distractions by taking the phone off the hook and letting your family know that you don't want to be disturbed unless it's an emergency.

- Use a padded mat to protect your spine.

- Barefoot is best. Socks otherwise.

- Clothing should be comfortable so that it does not restrict movement. Avoid belts, buckles and studs.

- Ensure you get into the habit of checking your alignment for each exercise. This will not only prevent injury, but also develop good, lifelong habits in everyday activities.

- Less is more! Pilates is about quality not quantity. The idea is that you bring all the Pilates principles into each movement. You will gain all the physical and mental benefits if you really focus on getting each movement correct without mindless repetition.

- Choose for yourself when to exercise, though the best times are in the late afternoon or evenings when your muscles are warmed up from the day's activities.

- Avoid eating heavy foods less than two hours before exercising.

- Ensure that you follow the instructions given for each movement. Don't be tempted to skip any of them, otherwise you will run the risk of performing them incorrectly, making them less effective and safe.

- Most importantly, remember Pilates should not cause pain. If pain other than the stretch sensation is experienced, stop immediately. You are either not performing the movement correctly or your body is not ready, so the movement needs to be modified.

When not to exercise

- If you are feeling unwell.

- If you have consumed alcohol.

- If you are on pain-killers as these will mask any warning signals.

- If you are under any medical treatment or are taking drugs. You must consult your medical practitioner first.

Summing Up

- Before you begin, read through the advice and information provided.

- Remember everything about Pilates is important. Take your time to understand the fundamentals and principles and put them into practice as these are the seed for growth.

- Try to form a regular routine in order to get more results and to develop the habit of practising regularly.

- Concentration is essential, especially as you begin to learn about your body and the movements. Be patient and get to know your body and how it works.

- Trust in the Pilates method. It works!

Chapter Two

The Pilates Principles

The following six principles are the underlying foundation of the whole Pilates method. They will act as a guide to your workout and are essential in bringing the full value to each and every movement.

Concentration

This is the first requirement. It is a very important principle and is crucial to each and every movement. Both mind and body participation is a requirement if you are going to get the full value from each exercise. Don't underestimate this principle and remember you are giving up your time to perform the movements; therefore, quality is essential throughout, otherwise you will lose the vital benefits of the exercise.

You will find that simple movements suddenly become a lot more complex when you concentrate on your whole body as you execute the exercises. This won't be easy initially, but in time and with patience it will become more straightforward. As you develop strong concentration skills, you are then better able to stop yourself from slipping into any bad habits. Also by concentrating you will have little room for other thoughts and anxieties – you will find your mind clears and becomes more focused, refreshed, alert and relaxed, which after a workout will serve you well in all other activities. Consider the following:

- Before you start and during each movement, check for correct alignment and position of every part of your body, not just your larger limbs but also your small ones such as your fingers and toes. Having one part of your body such as your head out of alignment will affect the rest of your body.

'You will find that simple movements suddenly become a lot more complex when you concentrate on your whole body as you execute the exercises.'

- Activate the correct muscles.

- Make sure you are performing the movement correctly by following the instructions and teaching points thoroughly.

Control

A motion without control can lead to injury. Every movement in Pilates should always be done with mindfulness in how you perform each and every exercise. It is important to move with quality, activating all the right muscles. In having control, you learn to work all your muscles, not just the strong ones but also the weaker ones, which can easily be missed if you are not controlling the movement. In fact, having control over the movements will actually give you more physical freedom. Initially, developing control will be a conscious act until it becomes more automatic. Think how beautiful athletes, dancers and animals such as cheetahs look. They have complete control. Consider the following:

'Make time for the fundamentals to help you find and engage the correct core muscles of the powerhouse.'

- Slow the movement down until you can gain full control and activate the correct muscles.

- Don't take any part of your body for granted otherwise some muscles will compensate for others, making the ones unused weaker.

- Modify a movement rather than forcing your body into a more advanced exercise, which will only do more harm than good. By working within your range, you will be able to control the movement better and execute it correctly.

Centring

We are working towards developing a strong centre by strengthening and firming the powerful torso muscles while keeping it supple. The centre, also referred to as the powerhouse, is from the bottom of the ribcage to the line across the hips, front and back of the body. There is a large group of muscles in our centre: the abdomen, lower back, hips and buttocks. Think about a girdle of strength wrapped around your body.

By building on our core strength, we gain more stability and control, creating a stable base with which our limbs, such as our arms and legs, can work from efficiently. It also acts as a natural corset for your vital organs, providing protection. Another positive side effect from focusing your attention on your torso is a trimmer waist and flatter stomach. You will also develop an elegant posture and move with more grace.

It is important to find and engage the correct muscles of the powerhouse every time you perform a movement. This engagement can be carried forward into everyday activities so that you can also help protect your back from strain and injury. In strengthening your centre, you will develop greater control when performing the movements and you will want to challenge yourself more by attempting the more advanced exercises. Consider the following:

- Make time for the fundamentals to help you find and engage the correct core muscles of the powerhouse.

- Concentrate on working from your centre as you perform the movements.

- Don't hold your breath as you engage your core muscles.

Flow

Joseph Pilates made the point that through practising his exercises you will develop grace, suppleness and skill that will be reflected in all that you do. Flowing movement is a re-education of body and mind that can be applied to our daily activities, which involve lots of transitions. There is no stop and start action – you should be flowing from one movement to the next from a strong centre, with all the muscles working together. The movements are controlled and continuous, not too slow or too fast, and the pace can be set by your own breathing. If you watch a professional dancer or an athlete, for example, they have an effortless flow and timing in their transitions and movements. Pilates is not about repeating a movement in a mindless motion but more about linking the movements together as one rather than six separate repetitions. Consider the following:

- Initially, slow the movement down to give yourself time to check that you are activating the right muscles and make sure that you are in a correct alignment in order to develop a safe and effective motion.

'Pilates is not about repeating a movement in a mindless motion but more about linking the movements together as one rather than six separate repetitions.'

- When you are using the right muscles, timing also plays a huge part in flowing movements. If the timing is late when activating the correct muscles then the smooth flowing motion will be jerky.

- Remember that stiff movements may be because of tight muscles. So until more suppleness and flexibility is gained through the continued practise of Pilates, flow may be hard to achieve initially.

Precision

Every movement in Pilates needs to be precise and by learning to activate the correct muscles you become more graceful. If precision is not maintained then the movements lose their value. Again, you are re-educating the mind as you train your mind to control the body in action. This will also bring benefits to your everyday activities. As you continue to bring your body back into correct alignment and learn to use it effectively, you will use less of your energy reserves, as this principle teaches you economy of movement. You will also become more aware of how you move and will develop more control and co-ordination. Nothing in Pilates is haphazard, therefore you are less likely to strain or fall if you have learned the valuable skill of precision. Consider the following:

'Every movement in Pilates needs to be precise and by learning to activate the correct muscles you become more graceful.'

- Try to be disciplined when you do Pilates, especially at the beginning. Over time it will become more automatic and feel more natural as you progress.

- Concentrate on activating the correct muscles. Bring your body back into correct alignment with accurate placement of every part of your body before and during the movements, until it becomes more automatic.

- A mirror will provide an opportunity for you to check for correct alignment and position at every stage of each movement.

- Remember, Pilates is about quality rather then quantity. The movements will be far more effective if you keep this in mind every time you workout.

Breath

Breathing is a very important part of Pilates. At the beginning, a lot of people find it difficult to get used to this. We develop poor breathing habits throughout our lives and Pilates will help correct these poor habits.

Breathing is very important as it increases stamina and energy. For our blood to do its job properly, it needs to be oxygenated; taking in oxygen on the breath in and then on the breath out emptying the lungs fully of carbon dioxide waste, cleansing our systems and getting our blood pumping.

Joseph Pilates said that above all else learn to breathe properly. The correct breathing habits learned in Pilates can then be carried forward into everyday activities. The breath when used properly will help you to release tension from the body, enabling you to manage life's pressures more effectively. Breathing correctly will also help you activate the correct muscles and develop rhythm to aid the flow and control of the exercises. Consider the following:

- Breathe in through the nose to filter dry, dirty and cold air. Breathe out through the mouth, expelling every single last bit of breath.

- Use the in breath at the point of effort and the out breath on the return of exhalation and relaxation.

- If you are doing something that tightens the body, squeeze air out of the lungs and inhale when straightening up.

- Feel where you take the breath to – Into the chest? Down to your tummy? Do your shoulders rise up as you breathe? Or can you feel the air expand to the sides of your ribs laterally and into your back and thoracic cavity? This latter description is the method used in Pilates.

'Joseph Pilates said that above all else learn to breathe properly.'

Summing Up

All six principles will in time become part of your Pilates practice. The first principle 'concentration' will be very important all the way through. You need to pay attention to your body before and during the movements, promoting union of mind and body. This will not be easy to start with but in time it will become easier and you will start to experience the other principles too. They will all make sense the more you progress in your Pilates practice.

Pilates when done properly will leave you wanting more rather than it being a chore. You will also find that all the principles can have a positive impact across your whole life.

Chapter Three

Knowing Your Body

It's very important to have knowledge about what a correct posture actually is and to assess your current posture and what you need to do to improve it. A basic understanding is required, otherwise you will have no guiding principle to work towards.

Body types

William Sheldon, an American psychologist who spent a lifetime observing and researching a variety of human bodies, stated that there are three basic human types.

Endomorph

Think of Jack Black or Roseanne.

- Larger than average.
- Softer and rounder.
- Due to the body shape the mass appears to be concentrated in the abdominal area and looks more like a pear shape.
- Can gain weight easily.

Ectomorph

Think of Kate Moss or Tom Hanks.

- Delicate build, muscles and bones.

- Lean and thin.
- Small shouldered.
- Takes longer to build muscle.

Mesomorph

Think of Sylvester Stallone or Demi Moore.

- Larger bones.
- Narrow and low waist.
- Well defined muscles and athletic.
- Gains muscles easily but can have poor flexibility.

We come in all shapes and sizes and although some people are purely one body type, very often we fall into mixed categories, therefore carrying one or two traits from the other body types.

'Our bodies require a healthy muscle structure for balance and function to maintain a good posture.'

Posture

Any body type can have good or bad posture. Our bodies require a healthy muscle structure to maintain a good posture. Correct alignment of the bones and joints allows the muscles to function properly. It is very important to have good posture not just while we exercise but in all that we do – whether we are standing, walking, sitting or lying down. We need to hold our bodies upright against gravity which is constantly pulling us down.

It's crucial to have a correct posture and alignment when practising Pilates and a good instructor will be able to help you achieve this. But it's also important for you to take responsibility for maintaining your concentration and awareness to achieve this too. This way you will get much more from the exercises without causing strain and pain during your workout. By committing to a regular practice of Pilates, you can pull your body back into correct alignment, as well as developing a healthy awareness of your body and how you hold yourself.

Spinal column basics

It's good to have a basic knowledge at least of the spinal column to help develop your awareness. The spine is a column that usually consists of 33 vertebrae. So here is an easy way to remember:

Cervical (your neck). The highest seven vertebrae, so try to remember as seven days of the week.

Thoracic (your neck to navel, or belly button). The next 12 vertebrae down associated with the 12 pairs of ribs, so remember as 12 months of the year.

Lumbar (your lower back). Five vertebrae down and the strongest and largest to support the lower back, so think of as five working days.

Sacrum (towards the bottom of the spine). Five which are vertebrae fused into one, again; think of as five working days.

Coccyx (your tail bone). This is made up of three to five vertebrae but with an average of four vertebrae, so remember as four weeks in a month (more or less!).

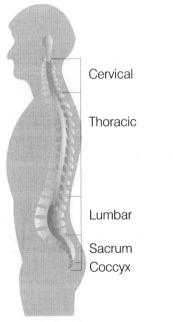

Cervical

Thoracic

Lumbar

Sacrum

Coccyx

'It's good to have a basic knowledge at least of the spinal column to help develop your awareness.'

Influences of bad posture

There are many great reasons to improve our posture to allow our bodies to function properly:

- Muscle balance, strength and tone.
- Protecting against joint aches and pains.
- Avoiding neck and shoulder tension.
- Improved circulatory system.
- Less tiredness and improved energy levels.
- Improved balance and co-ordination.
- Improved digestive system.
- Correct vital organ placement for maximum function.
- Elongated posture, improving appearance.

Here are some reasons that can explain poor posture:

Heredity

Our genetic makeup. This can determine our height and bone structure and so on.

Habit

Bad habits can accumulate over a lifetime through poor movement patterns. Therefore, muscle function becomes restrictive and imbalanced, causing further weakness which then affects our posture and alignment. We can pick up bad habits in our everyday activities.

Disease

Disease can affect the muscular and structural system which then alters your stance, limiting movement.

Nutrition

A poor diet can cause conditions that affect the bones and muscles.

Injury

Other muscles will compensate for the injured area. This then causes weakness and imbalance, leading to poor posture.

Improper shoes and clothes

Wearing shoes that don't fit properly or are worn down can affect how you hold yourself, causing poor posture. Even clothes that cause discomfort, such as the wrong size bra, can cause you to carry yourself differently to compensate for the discomfort.

Stress

Stress can affect our breathing. This can then cause tension and tightness in the body, leading us to hold our body in a negative way.

Attitude

Attitude can create good and bad posture. Someone who has a negative attitude tends to be bent over with slumped shoulders and knees hanging loosely, affecting posture in a negative way. But someone with a positive attitude tends to hold themselves in a strong upright position, with shoulders down and back.

Self-esteem

Poor self-esteem and body image can cause people to shrink by drooping their shoulders and upper body forwards with their head down, as though trying to disappear into the background and avoid being noticed.

Perfect posture

Pilates will help you find the ideal posture to help you to be as effective as you can in all that you do and to be protected against unnecessary pain. Unfortunately, if the posture fault is caused through disease or is hereditary, Pilates cannot cure this, although it will help to make your movement patterns better. If your posture fault is a muscular imbalance through lifestyle influences then, done correctly, Pilates can help you correct these faults. If you have a perfect posture and want to maintain this throughout life, Pilates will help you to achieve this too. A perfect posture means:

- Gravity across the whole body is evenly distributed.
- Muscle balance, making movement patterns normal.
- All joints are neutral.
- All vital organs are not restricted and can work at optimum levels.

The plumb line test

Plumb Line Test

Here is a good way to assess your posture. Stand sideways in front of a full length mirror wearing no clothes, or wear clothes that show your body shape. Imagine a heavy weighted piece of string hanging vertically. A perfect posture should be as follows with the string running down these points:

- Earlobe.

- Centre of the neck.

- Through the tip of the shoulder.

- Mid point of trunk of the body.

- Slightly in front of the centre of the knee joint.

- Finishing just in front of the ankle bone.

Postural types

A professional will be able to make an accurate assessment of your posture as it is not easy to tell which postural type you may or may not be. You may have the perfect posture, or perhaps some of the following faulty postures may be so subtle that only a trained eye would be able to spot them. You may even be a combination of all the postural types.

- Lordotic posture (lordosis).

- Flat back posture.

- Kyphotic posture (Kyphosis).

- Sway back posture.

- Scoliosis posture.

Here are some general posture type characteristics:

Lordosis

We all have a natural curve in our spine, but a lordotic spine is when there is an increased inward curve of the lower back. You may notice some of the following:

- Your abdominal muscles are stretched in this posture, making them weak and unable to effectively support the lower back.

- Your hamstrings are tight.

- Your bottom sticks out.

- Your pelvis is pulled forward.

- Your gut is protruding (think of someone who is pregnant or has a beer belly).

Flat back

This is where there is a reduced curve in the lower back and the spine appears to look straight. You may notice some of the following:

- Your head is forward of the plumb line.

- Your pelvis is tilted backwards.

- Your upper body is rounded, while the lower part of the spine appears straighter.

- You have tight and short hamstrings.

- Your knees are hyper-extended (locked) or they may be slightly flexed.

Kyphotic

This is an increased curve in the upper body part (thoracic spine). You may notice some of the following:

- A rounded upper body.

- Your head and chin poke forwards.

- Your pectoral (chest) muscles are tight.

- Your cervical spine is in hyperextension.

- Your thoracic spine is flexed.

- You slouch or have a hunchback appearance.

Sway back

This is where your hips are pushed forward and there is a forward tilt of the pelvis. The sway back can often be combined with lordosis and kyphotic posture types. You may notice some of the following:

- Your head is poking forward.

- Your pelvis is level but your hips are pushed forward.

- Your thoracic spine is leaning backwards.

- Your knees are hyper-extended.

- Your hamstrings are short and strong.

- Your gluteals (buttock muscles) are weak and wobbly.

Scoliosis

This is where there is an abnormal lateral (to the side) 'C' curve of the spine to either the left or the right, or it may be a double curve. This posture type can be muscular and can be caused through carrying heavy bags on one side for instance, which will then strengthen that side causing an imbalance. Or it may be hereditary.

- You may have a lateral curve in the lower spine or a lateral curve in the upper part (thoracic).

- You may notice a double curve 'S' shape.

Summing Up

You have an amazing body, but having more awareness of your body and posture type is essential if you are going to get the best improvements from exercise. It is also important to understand that a session of Pilates doesn't end in that session as you need to practise what you learn by taking it into your everyday life. Therefore, it is very important to be more aware of how your lifestyle can affect your body and how you move.

'You have an amazing body, but having more awareness of your body and posture type is essential if you are going to get the best improvements from exercise.'

Chapter Four

Body Awareness

Pilates is great for increasing your body awareness. You will become more aware of how you hold your body in movement and at rest.

It may feel awkward at first as you try to correct poor alignment, as over the years we can easily develop unhealthy habits. Therefore, the way you hold yourself now may feel more comfortable and normal, but in Pilates you will begin to unlearn these habits and relearn new, healthy ones. You will learn how to engage the correct muscles at the right time and develop an awareness of what every part of your body is doing before and during the movements. The attention is in the detail, so try to be patient as it will be more than worth it.

As you progress, you will strengthen your muscles, which will then help you form a tall and elegant posture without it feeling awkward and without having to consciously hold yourself in position. If I asked you now to sit up nice and tall, you would probably force your body into position, creating tension in your back. You are more likely to look like a soldier standing to attention! This is because you are used to letting your body fall into a comfortable position, allowing yourself to slouch or use the back of a chair for support, developing your muscles in the wrong way and creating weaknesses in your body. So, realistically, you wouldn't be able to hold this tall position for very long.

In Pilates, you will develop a strong and balanced body by using the correct muscles and strengthening them to support your body in all that you do – whether at rest or in movement. This will then enable you to develop a strong and healthy posture.

This chapter will help you understand the correct positions that are required during the practice of Pilates.

'Pilates is great for increasing your body awareness. You will become more aware of how you hold your body in movement and at rest.'

The Pilates box

Imagine drawing a perfect square box on your body. The line would be from shoulder to shoulder, then shoulder to hip, hip to hip, and then back up to your other shoulder. This is the Pilates box and is a powerful tool used to guide you in obtaining correct alignment and symmetry in everything that you do, whether practising Pilates or in everyday activities that we take for granted such as sitting at a computer, walking or driving a car. The Pilates box should be correct in movement and at rest.

Spine and pelvis position

We need to start with an ideal alignment before we perform the Pilates exercises. It will also promote strengthening of the abdominals, balance of muscles and correct muscle recruitment, thus avoiding tension and stress. The pelvis should not be tilted forward or back but in a natural, healthy position. To help you find the correct starting position, try this exercise:

- Lie down on your back on a padded mat and have your hands down by your sides, palms down and knees bent. Your legs and feet need to be hip width apart and the soles of your feet flat against the mat.

- Check that your earlobes, neck, shoulders and ribcage are aligned.

- Imagine you have two headlamps attached to your hip bones beaming up towards the ceiling in a straight line. This visualisation will help you to avoid tilting the hips out of alignment or extending them, which will arch your back off the floor.

- You will notice a natural curve in your spine.

- Now slide your feet as close as possible towards your buttocks, keeping them flat on the mat and knees bent.

- Can you feel the difference in the curve in your back? You should now feel your back is flatter against the mat.

- Now slide your feet halfway towards the start position. In this position you should now feel your back supported by the floor and there should be no tension anywhere in your body.

Neck and head position

Your head and neck position are also very important. If they are out of alignment, this will cause tension through your body and you will also be off balance. So starting with the head, consider the following guidelines:

- Lie on the mat and establish the correct spine and pelvis position. Then feel the base of your skull pressing towards the mat.

- The correct resting position is between the base of your skull and the top of your head.

- Your forehead should be parallel to the ceiling.

Now let's look at the correct position of your neck. There should be no pain or tension in the neck at any time and you should stop as soon as you feel any pain. You may experience pain and tension for many reasons – for example, if you are not in the correct alignment, if you are not performing the movement correctly or you are not ready for the movement. Therefore, you will need to regress until you are ready. This is the same for all the movements. So now your head is in alignment, let's consider your neck position:

- You want length in the back of your neck, so tilt your chin towards your chest without compression or squashing; keep it soft to avoid unnecessary tension leading to tight neck muscles.

- Imagine there is a piece of string attached to the crown of your head pulling you towards the wall behind you, or if standing, pulling you up towards the ceiling.

'Your head and neck position are also very important. If they are out of alignment then this will cause tension through your body and you will also be off balance.'

Shoulders

Stress and tension are a common factor in many people. If a friend or partner places their hands on your shoulders and massages them, the tension and tightness is immediately brought to your attention. You begin to feel them releasing and relaxing through the massage. Throughout the day we get wrapped up in all our chores and activities and we tend not to notice the tension building up in the shoulders as they hunch up around the ears.

A lot of our normal activities involve forward flexion such as working at a computer and driving. This shortens the chest muscles and moves the body out of correct alignment, leading to other problems such as back pain. In Pilates we are aiming to combat this as well as bringing awareness to how you hold yourself throughout the day, correcting unhealthy habits. But first let's bring our attention to what hunched shoulders look and feel like. Our aim is to feel space between the shoulders and ears and to keep them from curling forwards.

- Sit up nice and tall and imagine that piece of string pulling the crown of your head towards the ceiling.

- Now shrug both your shoulders high up towards your ears and then lower them down with control to create space between the shoulders and ears while relaxing the neck muscles.

- Now perform some shoulder rolls by rolling your shoulders back and down. Imagine the shoulder blades in a soft 'V' floating down towards your waistline.

Foot position

We often take our feet for granted. They are part of the body as a whole and play a very important part in how we move. When standing, we should evenly distribute our weight across the whole foot for balance. Think of a triangle at the bottom of your foot. The base of the triangle should run at the ball of the big toe to the outside edge of your foot, with the pointed part of the triangle at the centre of your heel.

When performing the exercises, it is very important to pay attention to your foot position as the position of your foot changes how the movement feels and the benefits you get from it. The foot shouldn't be left to flop around unattended. You will be instructed as to what foot position to take, but avoid over stretching and tightening the foot as this will not only throw you out of alignment, it can also lead to cramp. Think about lengthening and softly stretching into position. Here are the two foot positions that you will be given:

- Pointed – this is where you point the toes away from your head. Make sure that you don't crunch the bottom of the foot by curling the toes over.

- Flexed – this is where your heels should be further away from your head than the toes. Push your heels away from your body and bend the top of your feet back towards you (see the position of the feet in the illustration on page 75).

Buttocks

The buttock muscles (gluteals) are important in supporting our core strength and correct posture. Learning to use these muscles will not only firm and tone your bottom, but it will also make movement more powerful. Our gluteals play an integral part in many of the Pilates movements. You can also help tone and firm these muscles throughout the day by squeezing them together.

Seated position

Many people slump rather than sitting up nice and tall. Through the practice of Pilates, you will learn new healthy habits and will strengthen your muscles, which will make it easier to sit correctly. This not only looks so much nicer, but it will of course benefit your body. The following guidelines will help you:

- Think about sitting up out of your hips, tall on your seat bones.
- Imagine that you have two £50 notes under your seat bones and you don't want them to blow away.
- Now imagine that you have a pole attached to your spine, neck and head. Lengthen up along this pole, drawing your lower tummy muscles in and up as if reaching towards your spine.
- Imagine that a piece of string is attached to the crown of your head drawing you up towards the ceiling, keeping length in the back of the neck.
- Now lift your chest towards the ceiling while sliding your spine up the imaginary pole which will help you to avoid arching your back.

Lengthening

Always think about lengthening in Pilates. This is why Pilates develops lean muscles without the bulk. Also by lengthening while performing the movements, stress is reduced on our joints and mobility of the joints is increased. It can be more challenging to elongate the body while doing the exercises, but it is important for efficient movement. For instance, even when we are lifting into a forward flexion position in our upper body from the mat, you should still think of lengthening through the curled up position, not crunching. The following guidelines will help you:

- Think about stretching from your arm and leg sockets.

- Lengthen without hyperextending your elbows and knees as this will cause tension and stress on the joints.

- Aim for the straightest line possible, taut and long.

'Always think about lengthening in Pilates. This is why Pilates develops lean muscles without the bulk.'

Summing Up

It may seem like a lot to take in, but don't worry. In time and with a bit of patience, everything will make sense and become more natural to you.

As you have seen from this chapter, the position of your body does make a huge difference to the quality of all the Pilates movements. Your re-education of your body will also benefit how you move throughout the day in all that you do. For instance, your increased awareness will bring you to pay more attention to your shoulders – are they hunched up and tense? You will learn to relax them down. What about how you sit at your computer – are you sitting tall out of your hips and on your seat bones? One of the many advantages of knowing how to correct yourself as you sit at the computer is that you will develop a stronger posture, helping you to avoid developing back pain in the future.

So, as you can see, the practice of Pilates really will help you to develop new healthy habits and will also improve how you feel.

Chapter Five

About the Exercises

In this chapter we will discuss what you can expect when looking at the information provided for each exercise. I know it can feel like a slow process as you try to understand the instructions and it can become a little frustrating, but try to imagine you are having a one-to-one session with an instructor. You wouldn't want the instructor to rush through things to save themselves some time would you? This would mean that they were selling you short. The same principle applies to this book. If you are to truly learn the Pilates method and gain the many benefits that made you buy this book in the first place, then every time you workout think of it as if you are paying for a private session. I can assure you that your time and patience will be rewarded. Just trust the method and it will work for you like it has for many others.

The instructions

All the instructions and teaching points are important. Do the exercises in the order in which they are set out as they are designed to flow from one exercise to another. Read through them until you feel confident about what it is you have to do. Pay special attention to the teaching points as these will be helpful in making sure that you perform the movement correctly.

The exercises will lose their value if they are not done correctly. However, please don't worry though; it will take time to get the exercises spot on. All I ask is that you persevere with that goal in mind and you will see and feel a difference. Pilates is about quality of the movement, not quantity. The information will be laid out in a simple, step-by-step style as follows:

- The exercise and the objectives.
- The instructions.

- Helpful visualisations.
- The teaching points – very important!

After reading all the information provided, you can then attempt the exercise. This is likely to highlight some difficulties, as actually doing them is quite challenging, so don't be surprised if you need to refer back to the instructions again to check that you are on the right track.

Modifications

'Try to visualise the movement in your mind. Then visualise it again and try to think about applying the Pilates principles to that visualisation.'

Always start with the modifications no matter how fit you are, as starting at this stage will help you get the technique correct. There is a lot more to the exercises than just being able to do them. Pilates is a thinking exercise system which is why it benefits both mind and body.

Don't move on until you have mastered the modified versions confidently without struggling and without having to refer to the instructions (although it's always good to remind yourself of the instructions now and again to stop yourself from falling into bad habits!). Already you will have used the concentration principle because, as you will have experienced, there is a lot to think about when doing Pilates. Try to incorporate all six Pilates principles into every movement. Challenge yourself – but remember, you should never feel any pain as this is definitely not a 'no pain, no gain' system.

The term 'work within your range of movement' simply means that you should not push yourself beyond your current level of strength and flexibility. As you progress in your Pilates practice, you will find that your range of movement will significantly improve.

Illustrations

The illustrations will help you to form a mental picture of what the movement looks like. Try to visualise the movement in your mind. Then visualise it again and try to think about applying the Pilates principles to that visualisation. This will help you to become familiar with these principles as you do the exercise. It's important to remind yourself that the principles are there to guide you in performing the movements correctly, so that you then gain all the vital benefits from doing them.

Important point

Not all the illustrations show all the exercises that are described. So it is crucial that you read all the instructions provided for each progression.

The breathing pattern

Many people find that they get confused with the breathing pattern when they perform the movement. Although breathing is a fundamental principle in the Pilates method, please don't get into a panic over it. You will be instructed as to what the correct breathing pattern is for each exercise.

You will find as I did when I first started (and as do many others) that it takes a lot of your concentration to get the movement and your alignment correct, let alone breathe at the right time too. So just begin by making sure, at the very least, that you are not holding your breath. This may sound silly, but it is a common fault – we can forget to breathe when we are concentrating hard on what we are doing, making the breath shallow and inadequate. In time, you will grasp the correct breathing pattern as you become more familiar with the exercises, and you will use it to your advantage. Just take your time and refer back to the breathing principle to help you understand the general rule.

The term 'in breath to prepare' used in the exercise instructions simply means that on the in breath you should breath into the sides and back of your ribcage, all the way down to your spine and into your pelvic bowl. Ensure your shoulders are back and down away from your ears and your neck is tension free.

Helpful visualisations

Imagery is a valuable tool when doing Pilates. Using imagery is there to help you to better understand the movement, rather than going into great detail technically. Visualisation can immediately give you a 'light on' understanding of what the movement should look and feel like. For instance, previously to help you understand the correct seated position, I said to imagine a pole attached to your spine, neck and head. I also talked about a piece of string being attached to the crown of your head, drawing you up towards the ceiling. Both these images provide an immediate mental picture and feeling of lengthening upwards in the correct way.

Teaching points

Every Pilates exercise along with the instructions will also have teaching points. These teaching points are there to keep you on the right track and to help you avoid the common pitfalls. They will remind you of the correct alignment required for a movement, for example: maintain length in the back of the neck, keep your shoulders relaxed and down away from your ears. These points are a quick read and will shine a light on the important points that are essential for you to execute the movement correctly.

Repetitions

When we talk about Pilates, less is definitely more! Joseph Pilates spoke of mindless repetitions being completely unnecessary in his method of exercise. By repeating the same movement over and over again, the movement goes from being mindful to mindless. It becomes boring and you begin to lose focus and the body compensates by allowing the stronger muscles to take over, causing an imbalance. Therefore, the movement loses its value, which if you have read this book up to now, you know that to get the best results from the Pilates method all the exercises must be done with precision, which takes a lot of concentration. Having this precision means that you recruit the correct muscles to the maximum. This makes the exercises highly effective without wear and tear on the body.

'Joseph Pilates spoke of mindless repetitions being completely unnecessary in his method of exercise. By repeating the same movement over and over again, the movement goes from being mindful to mindless.'

Summing Up

This chapter has provided you with plenty of preparation to help you appreciate how important it is to follow the instructions and teaching points for each and every Pilates movement. The Pilates method may seem like a lot to take in at first, but once you begin to become familiar with the method, you will really appreciate and enjoy the many benefits that it promises to deliver. Soon, rather than thinking about your workout as a chore, you will really look forward to your session of Pilates. Try to get into a regular routine of doing your Pilates workout as this will help to develop and condition you both mentally and physically. Also you will find that once you have learned the routine thoroughly, it really will not take much time out of your day to do it and will have far reaching benefits.

Chapter Six

The Fundamentals of Pilates

This chapter introduces you to the fundamentals – the basic exercises and information will be great preparation before moving onto the main programme. How to practise these fundamentals will be explained in the next chapter.

It will also be worth returning to these fundamentals later on to check your alignment and correct core muscle engagement to ensure that you are getting the maximum benefits from your workout.

Roll downs

The roll down is a good exercise to start your session before beginning your main workout programme. However, it isn't for everyone and you should seek professional advice if you have a back problem. Later on in chapter 7 you will be shown how to perform this movement against a wall, and then you can progress to doing this movement free standing.

The wall is a modified version and will offer support for your weight and will provide you with tactile feedback as you begin to learn segmental control. Segmental control involves peeling your spine vertebrae by vertebrae away from the wall and then restacking vertebrae by vertebrae back up against the wall. Try to create length between each vertebrae as you go.

Joseph Pilates didn't like abrupt movements with the back and encouraged his students to roll up and down like a wheel. Therefore, try and visualise your vertebrae attached to the rim of a wheel as you lift and lower yourself to the mat. Benefits to the roll down include:

'The roll down is a good exercise to start your session with before beginning your main workout programme.'

- It encourages segmental control – rolling down and up in a safe and controlled way. In fact, it's a good way of lowering yourself to the mat ready for your workout.

- It mobilises the spine and promotes correct alignment.

- It releases pressure in the spine, shoulders and upper body.

- It's good for finding and engaging the correct core muscles, as you will be using these when controlling the roll down and up in the correct alignment.

- It helps to focus the mind ready for your session.

Starting position

It is very important to establish a correct starting position. This will provide you with a safe and effective position before each and every exercise (refer to spine and pelvis postion on page 30 and compass work on page 56).

Relax and why?

As strange as it may sound, it's a good idea to relax before you begin your Pilates, as it is natural to bring the stress of the day into your session. Therefore, it is important to give yourself the time to bring your attention into the room before you start by letting go of what's happened or going on outside. It only need take a few minutes as you scan your whole body for any tension and then allow that tension to melt away into the floor.

You will get far more from the exercises if you start with an inner focus and without tension, which encourages tightening up of the muscles. This is a healthy habit to develop as it's good to develop awareness of when tension begins to build up and to learn to release it. For instance, if you are sat at your computer screen, you will begin to recognise the feeling of your shoulders creeping up around your ears and so learn to release them down. You may also begin to notice that when you are driving you are holding the steering wheel tightly which will create tension in your body. If you become more

'You will get far more from the exercises if you start with an inner focus and without tension.'

switched on to when tension and stress is building up, you will then be able to release and let go. Otherwise all these situations will have a negative effect on you both mentally and physically.

Breathing

Breathing helps the body and mind to cope with stress. Joseph Pilates said in his book, *Return to Life Through Contrology*, 'Since we cannot live without breathing it is tragically deplorable to contemplate the millions and millions who have never learned to master the art of correct breathing.'

Not only is this a guiding Pilates principle, it is also essential to good health. Your body will be nourished through proper breathing. As you fully exhale, squeezing every last bit of breath from the body, your lungs will automatically refill with fresh air, oxygenating your blood stream and preventing fatigue. The goal of Pilates is to encourage natural and effortless breathing so that you can carry this through to everyday life.

Core stability

In Pilates, core stability awareness is developed so that we can learn to use our core muscles correctly. The muscles will also become stronger which is very important for supporting your back and keeping you upright. If you relax your abdominal muscles, you will feel your body collapse, but if you learn to engage them, you will feel your body lengthening upwards in a supported upright position. The abdominals consist of four layers of elastic crisscrossing bands of muscle fibres which provide stability and mobility to the spine and pelvis and enable you to stand upright, move limbs and support your organs. There are four abdominal groups as follows.

Rectus abdominis

These muscles run vertically in front of the body from the sternum (the bone in the middle of your chest, also referred to as the 'breast bone') to the pelvis. These muscles can be seen; think of a six pack. They are important for maintaining posture.

'In Pilates, core stability awareness is developed so that we can use our core muscles correctly.'

External and internal obliques

The external obliques run diagonally just below the sternum and wrap around the waist. The internal obliques are underneath them and run diagonally from the lower ribs to the pelvis. Both sets of obliques are used in twisting and bending the body.

Transversus abdominis

These are the deepest layers of muscle in the abdominals and are part of the deep postural muscle group. They wrap around the waist to the back and down in front of the hips towards the pelvis. In Pilates you will strengthen these muscles, which will not only help you achieve a flatter tummy, but will also provide support and stability to the lower back and can support the position of the pelvis.

'Think of the deep postural muscles as a corset. This corset provides the support and power to your body.'

The deep postural muscles

Think of the deep postural muscles as a corset. This corset provides the support and power to your body. The top of the corset is the diaphragm. Then the transverses abdominis, as described above, wrap around from the back to across the abdominals below the navel like a belt buckle. The back of the corset is the multifidus muscle and the muscle at the bottom of the corset is the pelvic floor muscle. In Pilates you will learn to find and engage these deep postural muscles and this should be carried forwards into your everyday life so that you can support and protect your back, as well as providing a stable base for your body to work from at its very best.

These muscle groups are responsible for stabilising the trunk while you move. If, for example, you reached up to get something out of cupboard, these deep postural muscles are recruited first to stop you falling. These muscles help to provide a girdle of strength so that everyday movement can be carried out safely and smoothly. Think of the inner layer of a tree trunk. If the trunk of a tree was empty and hollow on the inside then without much force it would collapse. That's why these muscles are crucial for inner strength. The Pilates method works from the inside out to create a stable base to work from.

Now let's look at the diaphragm, multifidus and pelvic floor muscles.

Diaphragm muscle

We have already discussed the use of the breath in Pilates. Where you send the breath, influences the muscles you use. Breathing correctly helps to promote the plumb line posture and helps develop the muscles in the entire torso. The diaphragm muscle resembles a dome shape which attaches underneath the ribcage and helps you to breathe. It may help to imagine breathing air in and out of a two way vacuum.

Multifidus muscle

This small but powerful muscle is a series of muscles attached to the spinal column. These deep muscles contribute significantly to the stability of the spine. They work in co-activation with the transverse abdominis and are recruited during many actions in our daily living, such as bending backward, sideways and even turning our body to the sides. They provide support to the vertebrae and ultimately the whole spine with muscle activation.

Pelvic floor muscles

In order to achieve the best possible stability, it is important to be able to contract the pelvic floor muscles at the same time as engaging the transverse abdominal muscles. To help you locate these muscles, imagine stopping urination mid-flow.

Compass work

This is a helpful exercise when trying to find the correct position of the spine and pelvis. It is also a great way to create mobility in the pelvis and to explore the full range of pelvic mobility. The compass work will enable you to feel the difference between creating movement in the pelvis and then stabilising the pelvis when you come to the correct starting position. When on the mat, imagine a compass on your lower tummy; north being the navel (belly button) and south being the pubic bone.

It is very easy when engaging the lower abdominals to tilt or tuck the pelvis and you want to avoid this as it's important to start in a level pelvic position. It also helps to imagine that you have a bowl of water balancing on your lower tummy and you must avoid spilling any of it. To do this, you will need to have a level pelvic position to keep the bowl balanced on your tummy.

Pelvic curls

'The pelvic curl is a great movement for creating mobility and flexibility in your spine, which is good preparation for your Pilates practice.'

The pelvic curl is a great movement for creating mobility and flexibility in your spine, which is good preparation for your Pilates practice. This exercise will also help you to recruit the correct deep postural muscles which will help you to control the movement. It also teaches segmental control rather than abrupt motions as you lift and lower off the mat from the supine position (lying down with the face up). This movement will teach you to lift vertebrae by vertebrae off the mat, creating length between each vertebrae as you lift and lower.

Some Pilates teachers use the image of a bicycle chain to describe the movement of the spine. Alternatively, some people find it easier to think of imprints in the sand; as you lower back down to the mat, imagine placing your vertebrae one by one neatly back into the imprints again. You will only start with small movements and then when your range of movement and strength increases you will gradually go from pelvic tilts to a ski slope position. So on this occasion it is probably best to remove that imaginary bowl of water, otherwise you will get a very wet tummy!

Knee folds

This exercise is great for getting you started and improves pelvic stability. By starting with a small and simple movement like this, you learn how to correctly stabilise the pelvis while your legs move. The knee folds will also develop your awareness of the powerhouse as you learn to engage and activate the correct muscles. As you raise and lower your legs, you will develop more awareness of how this subtle movement affects your pelvis. The goal of this exercise is to maintain stability in your pelvis rather than allowing it to wobble around from side to side. You will then begin to learn how to engage your lower tummy muscles in order to help you control the movement and to help keep your pelvis stabilised as you raise and lower your legs.

Supine spinal rotation

Spinal rotation is a fundamental skill required for many of the Pilates movements as well as many daily activities. This exercise will help you to achieve spinal rotation with stability and bring awareness to your oblique muscles. As you rotate your lower body from side to side, you will find that by contracting your lower tummy muscles you learn how to maintain greater stability and improve movement patterns in your body. This will provide an increasingly flexible range of movement in your spine and greater abdominal control. Your range of movement will depend on your current flexibility and abdominal strength. Therefore, as with all the exercises, your range of movement will improve as your Pilates practice progresses.

Ribcage and shoulder stability

This is also a fundamental skill required for the Pilates movements. A good muscular connection from the ribcage to the shoulder girdle is essential for good movement. So by maintaining ribcage and shoulder girdle stability, you can reach and lift your arms and shoulders away from the body in a healthy and safe motion. Ribcage stability is also important in enabling you to maintain a strong centre and is needed for a good alignment of the ribs to the pelvis. Shoulder stability is also important while performing the more challenging Pilates movements.

'A good muscular connection from the ribcage to the shoulder girdle is essential for good movement.'

Upper body flexion

This curl up movement will develop strength in the abdominals, helping you to engage the correct deep postural muscles and increase your range of movement in your upper spine. The curl ups will help prepare you for when you perform some of the Pilates movements later on.

In this movement you will lift your head, shoulders and upper body off the mat from the supine position (lying on your back) without any pulling on the neck. The curl up should always start from the correct recruitment of the powerhouse muscles. You should also ensure that you lengthen into the upward curl rather than crunching forwards. The pace should be slower, eliminating momentum to increase intensity. This will also give you the chance to make sure that you use the right muscles and maintain pelvic stability. A common mistake when you are new to Pilates is to tilt your pelvis towards your head as you curl up. To help you avoid this, use the visualisation of a bowl of water balancing on your lower abdominals; if you tilted your pelvis towards your head, the water would spill all over your tummy.

Rest position and roll up to standing

'The rest position provides a great way to relax and allows the spine to stretch and it can be done at any time during your workout.'

The rest position provides a great way to relax and allows the spine to stretch and it can be done at any time during your workout. The other reason I have included the rest position is that it offers a useful transition from the mat up to a standing position. As you roll up to standing, you will slowly uncurl your spine using segmental control until you reach an upright position.

Summing Up

The fundamental introduction has now hopefully given you a better understanding of why they are important before putting them into practice in the following chapter.

It is important that you know the fundamentals as they will enable you to get the best out of your exercises and help in preparing your body for the main workout. They will also give your workout more depth as the basics are crucial building blocks for your main workout routine.

Chapter Seven

Putting the Fundamentals into Practice

Now that you have been introduced to the basic fundamentals, it's time to put them into practice. Take your time and make sure you read all the instructions. If you don't get it straightaway, don't worry – it does take time, so be patient with yourself.

Breathing

Aim

- To establish correct breathing habits as you workout and then apply this to everyday life for health and vitality.

How

- Place your hands on the front of your ribcage, fingertips touching.
- Breathe in through your nose – you should feel and see some parting of your fingers. As you breathe out through your mouth, your fingers should come back together again. Remember to keep your shoulders relaxed and down.

If you find it difficult then try this method instead or, better still, try them both.

- Wrap a scarf around your ribs, crossing it over at the front and holding the ends of your scarf. Pull it tightly, keeping your shoulders relaxed and down.

- As you breathe in, you should be able to feel your ribs expand against the material as the ribcage moves upward and outward. Aim to allow the breath to fully expand into the sides and back of your ribcage and all the way down to your pelvic bowl.

- As you breathe out, you should feel your ribcage move downwards and inwards.

Starting and relaxation position

Aim

- To establish a healthy starting position.

- To bring focus to your Pilates session.

- To learn to let go of any tension and stress.

How

- Carefully and safely lower yourself down to the mat by bending one knee to the floor followed by your second knee. Then turn over and come to a seated position with your legs in front of you, knees bent, feet flat against the mat. Place your hands around the back of your thighs as you create a 'C' curve in your spine and gently roll your spine backwards, vertebrae by vertebrae down towards the mat to the starting position. You can use a small, firm and flat cushion to place under your head if this is more comfortable for you.

- Keep your knees bent with feet and legs hip width apart, with the soles of your feet flat against the mat.

- Lengthen the back of your neck by tilting your chin towards your chest, leaving just enough room for a small peach between your chin and chest. Feel the base of your skull pressing towards the mat with your forehead parallel to the ceiling.

- Arms down by your sides, palms facing down.

- Shoulders relaxed down away from your ears with your shoulder blades in a soft 'V' floating down towards your waist in your back. Keep your shoulder blades in contact with your mat.

- Maintain a level pelvis and spine (see spine and pelvis position, page 30).

- Body scan yourself starting from your toes and feet, all the way up to your head. Consciously relax each body part towards the floor. Feel the tension being released and allow it to melt away into the floor.

- Use gentle but full breaths in through the nose and out through the mouth. You can place your hands on your lower ribcage and feel your ribs expand as you breathe in and your ribs closing together as you breathe out.

Visualisation

Imagine the mat is a sponge and absorbs all the tension away from your body.

Teaching points

- Try to close off any outside distractions such as being interrupted by family members and put your phone on silent.

- Try to pick a certain time of day when you are less likely to have interruptions.

Compass work

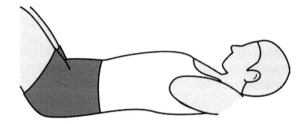

Aim

- To develop awareness of the range of movement in your pelvis.

- To find the correct starting position – level pelvis and spine.

How

- Lie down on the mat in the starting position and check your alignment is correct.

- Imagine a compass on your tummy. Your navel being north and your pubic bone being south.

- Gently tilt your pubic bone northward towards your navel. You will notice when you do this that the curve in the lower back is lost.

- Next gently tilt your navel southward, back towards your pubic bone. You will now notice your lower back arching off the floor and your ribs flaring upwards.

- Learn to feel the difference it makes to your back when tilting your pelvis backwards and forwards. Now let the pelvis come back to the centre by making the movements between north and south smaller and smaller until you arrive at the neutral, level position. This should be neither too far north nor too far south, with the tailbone remaining on the floor lengthening away. Try to maintain this neutral position when lying, standing, sitting or side lying.

- Use gentle but full breaths throughout.

Visualisation

Imagine a compass on your lower tummy. Then as you bring your pelvis level into a correct starting position imagine the pointer being level between north and south. It can also help to imagine that you have headlamps attached to your hips with the beam of light reaching in a straight line towards the ceiling.

Teaching points

- The movements should be small and gentle.
- Don't strain by over extending the arch from north to south or by crunching from south to north.
- Keep your upper body still without tension and shoulders relaxed down away from your ears.
- Maintain navel to spine throughout (refer to the next section below for instructions on how to do this).

Core stability

Aim

- To find and engage your core stability muscles, which is crucial for all the Pilates movements as well as taking this on through to everyday activities.

How

The term 'navel to spine' will be used in the instructions for the exercises and this term is used to remind you to engage your core stability muscles deep in your tummy. This is essential in strengthening your torso and protecting your spine as you move your body.

- Lie on the mat in the starting position and check your alignment is correct.

- Breathe naturally and imagine you have a piece of string attached to your navel, and the string is pulling your navel down towards your spine, as if drawing your lower tummy muscles in and up.

- On the out breath, hold that contraction for five to 10 seconds and continue to breathe normally. Then release the contraction.

Repeat three or four times and aim to master normal breathing while maintaining the contraction in your lower tummy comfortably.

Visualisation

Imagine there is some string attached to your navel pulling it down towards your spine as if closing the gap between your navel and spine.

Teaching points

- Keep a level spine. Do not tilt the pelvis out of alignment.

- When drawing in the tummy muscles, do not make the common mistake of sucking in your stomach which will only cause you to hold your breath. Instead, imagine a heavy weight pressing down on your tummy towards the spine.

Pelvic tilts into pelvic curls

Aim

- To mobilise your spine and warm up for the exercises.

- Teach segmental control – 'vertebrae by vertebrae'.

Stage one – how

- Lie on the mat in the starting position and check your alignment is correct.

- In breath to prepare, breathe wide and full into your ribcage.

- On the out breath, navel to spine and tilt your pelvis towards you, curling your tailbone and lower buttocks very slightly off the mat. Keep your lower back on the mat throughout.
- On the in breath, lower back down to the mat to the starting position.
- Repeat four or five times.

Stage two – progression

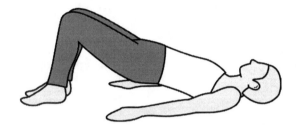

Increase your range of movement gradually to progress into the pelvic curl movement, vertebrae by vertebrae as you lift from to the mat until eventually you reach a ski slope shape on the front of your body without arching your back.

- In breath to prepare.
- On the out breath, navel to spine and begin to curl your pelvis off the mat.
- On the in breath, maintain navel to spine and hold still in the ski slope position.
- On the out breath, tuck your tail bone up as you lower yourself down to the mat, vertebrae by vertebrae back to the starting position.

Visualisation

Imagine that your spine is like a surface of a tyre, every part touches the road as it goes round. Or try to imagine pulling a string of beads from a silk box – bead by bead (vertebrae by vertebrae) – and then laying them back down again in the silk box, bead by bead (vertebrae by vertebrae).

Teaching points

- Do not arch your back.

- Keep your upper body still and your shoulders and neck relaxed.

- Lift and lower yourself to the mat vertebrae by vertebrae.

- Keep your pelvis from tipping to one side by engaging your core muscle strength for stability and balance.

- Keep length in the back of your neck.

- Keep your knees stable – you can place a pillow between your knees for guidance.

- Only work within your range of movement by lifting only as far as you can while maintaining the quality of the movement.

- Maintain navel to spine throughout.

Knee folds

Aim

- To develop pelvic stability while your limbs are moving.

- To teach correct engagement of your core muscles.

- To develop a mind and body connection.

How

- Lie on the mat in the starting position and check your alignment is correct.

- In breath to prepare, breathe wide and full into your ribcage.

- On the out breath, draw your lower tummy muscles in and up (navel to spine) and raise one leg to a table top position.

- On the in breath, lower your leg slowly back down to the mat without any pressure on your foot and imagine just dipping your toe into a stream before raising the same leg back up again to table top position on the out breath.

- Repeat three times before changing to your other leg.

Visualisation

Imagine a bowl of water balancing on your lower tummy – try not to spill any of it! You could also imagine that your legs are feather-light.

Teaching points

- Engage your lower tummy muscles before raising and lowering your leg.

- Keep your pelvis in neutral position by not tilting the pelvis – think about the compass pointer being level between north and south with headlamps on your hips reaching up towards the ceiling in a straight beam of light.

- Keep your upper body still.

- Maintain length in the back of your neck and keep your shoulders down with your shoulder blades in a soft 'V' shape.

- Keep the movement slow and controlled.

- Maintain navel to spine throughout.

Supine spinal rotation

Aim

- To teach spinal rotation with stability. This is an important skill for many of the Pilates movements and for everyday activities too.
- To work the obliques.

How

- Lie on the mat in the starting position and check your alignment is correct.
- Bring your legs and feet gently together with the soles of your feet flat against the mat. Your arms down by your sides, palms facing down.
- On the in breath, navel to spine as you slowly roll your knees gently to the right. Take them only within your range of movement and keep your ribs and shoulders anchored towards the mat. Your left hip and foot will rise off the mat slightly.
- On the out breath, navel to spine and bring your legs, spine and pelvis back to the centre.
- Repeat on the other side.
- Repeat three times each side.

Visualisation

Feel the movement as you twist and untwist.

Teaching points

- Don't arch your back off the mat and keep your shoulders relaxed and still.
- Feel each vertebrae as it rolls on and off the mat.

- Keep the movement small and flowing and keep your knees and feet together without letting them slide around.

- Use your core abdominal strength to control the movement – navel to spine should be maintained throughout.

- Keep your shoulder blades in contact with the mat.

Upper body – shoulder and ribcage stability

Aim

- To develop the skill of moving the upper body correctly, while stabilising your centre as your arms and shoulders move.

Stage one – how

- Lie on the mat in the starting position and check your alignment is correct.

- On the in breath, navel to spine and raise one arm towards the ceiling.

- On the out breath, navel to spine and slowly lower your arm behind you towards the mat above your head. Only take your arm back within your range of movement and feel your shoulder blades sliding down your back. Use core stability and the out breath to stabilise your ribcage. Stop the movement when your ribs begin to flare up towards the ceiling.

- On the in breath, bring your arm back up towards the ceiling. Then on the out breath, lower it again back towards the mat behind you.

- Repeat this action five more times before repeating with your other arm.

Stage two – progression

- If you have achieved the correct movement with one arm at a time, try this movement with both arms together.

Visualisation

Imagine that your shoulder blades are in oil, sliding down your back as you lower them behind you towards the mat. Or you could imagine you have a glass of water balancing on your ribcage. This will help you to avoid allowing your ribcage to flare up towards to the ceiling, causing you to arch your back off the mat.

Teaching points

- Keep your shoulder blades down and in contact with the mat.
- Stop when any further movement causes your ribcage to flare up and your back to arch off the mat.
- Use your core stability muscles by maintaining navel to spine, stabilising your centre.
- Do not strain or force your arm back – only work within your range of movement.
- Keep your elbows soft.

Curl ups

If you suffer with neck problems then you should seek medical advice before attempting this exercise.

Aim

- To develop abdominal strength.
- To teach you upper body flexion, recruiting the correct core stability muscles. Upper body flexion is a skill required for many of the Pilates exercises.

How

- Lie on the mat in the starting position and check your alignment is correct.

- Place one hand behind your head and place your other hand on your lower abdomen.

- In breath to prepare, breathe wide and full into ribcage.

- On the out breath, draw your lower tummy muscles in and up – navel to spine and curl your upper body up off the mat vertebrae by vertebrae, lengthening into a curl, not crunching forwards. Keep the tips of your shoulder blades in contact with the mat and chin towards your chest.

- On the in breath, deepen navel to spine.

- On the out breath, slowly lower your upper body vertebrae by vertebrae back down to the mat.

- Repeat three times more and then swap over hands.

Visualisation

Imagine a small bunch of grapes on your abdomen. You want to avoid crushing them as you curl up.

Teaching points

- Do not pull on your neck. Use your abdominal core strength to raise and lower.

- Only work within your range of movement. Do not strain.

- Lengthen into the curl up. Do not crunch into forward flexion.

- Raise and lower vertebrae by vertebrae.

- Control the movement by slowing it down and using core stability strength.

- Do not tilt your pelvis towards your tummy (south to north) as you curl up.

- Your hand on your tummy is there to check that it is not popping up.

- Maintain navel to spine throughout.

Rest position and roll up to standing

It is best to avoid the rest position if you suffer with knee problems. As an alternative, you can lie on your side in the foetal position.

Aim

- This exercise can be done anytime but is especially recommended after lying on your front such as after performing the swan dive exercise (see page 93).

- To rest and stretch your back, this position is also a good transition into the other exercises or rolling up to a standing position.

How

- Come onto all fours and either bring your toes together and keep your knees apart to get an extra inner thigh stretch or bring your legs together for more of a back stretch. The first option is recommended if you have a back injury.

- Slowly drop your buttocks back onto your heels and rest your forehead on the mat with your arms out in front, palms down. Or you can choose to bring your arms down by your sides and let your knuckles rest on the mat, depending on your comfort preference.

- From this rest position, navel to spine and come back onto all fours.

- Curl your toes under and walk your hands back along the mat towards your knees and slowly uncurl your spine vertebrae by vertebrae maintaining navel to spine as you come into an upright standing position.

Need2Know

Visualisation

Think of how a cat or a dog eases back into a stretch, nothing is forced.

Teaching points

- Just relax into the stretch.
- Avoid any tension in the neck.

Roll downs

Seek advice from a healthcare professional if you suffer with back and neck problems before attempting the roll down movement. First, start off against the wall and then when you are familiar with the movement and are physically able, you can progress to doing a free standing roll down.

Aim

- To warm up and release tension in the spine and is good preparation for the rest of the exercises.
- To develop awareness of alignment and balance.

- To teach segmental control – vertebrae by vertebrae.
- To teach correct engagement of your core stability muscles.
- To provide a good way to lower yourself down to the mat.

Stage one – how

- Stand against a wall, placing your feet 12 to 24 feet away from the wall (depending on your height).
- Your feet should be hip width apart and your knees bent – imagine you are sitting on a bar stool.
- You should feel your tailbone and pubic bone reaching towards the floor.
- In breath to prepare, breathe wide and full into your ribcage.
- On the out breath, navel to spine, start by tilting your chin to your chest with length in the back of your neck (you should feel the stretch at the back of your neck).
- Roll down away from the wall vertebrae by vertebrae, beginning with the weight of your head, arms relaxed down with your finger tips reaching towards the floor and neck relaxed. Maintain navel to spine throughout.
- Only roll down within your range of movement, keeping buttocks against the wall.
- On the in breath, hold a relaxed but not slumped position at the bottom.
- On the out breath, navel to spine as you articulate your spine back up against the wall vertebrae by vertebrae until you reach the upright position that you started with.

Stage two – progression

You should only attempt free standing roll downs when you are ready, having mastered the roll down against a wall.

- Take an in breath to prepare. Mentally check correct alignment, think about the plumb line test from earlier.

- On the out breath, roll down as instructed before, only taking it within your range of movement. Knees should be soft. If you have tight hamstrings then bend them slightly.

- Take an in breath at the bottom.

- On the out breath, uncurl the spine vertebrae by vertebrae back up to an upright position. In the upright position, mentally reassess your alignment.

- Repeat three to six times.

Visualisation

Imagine your spine is a bicycle chain as you roll down and back up. Or if free standing, as you haven't got a wall to provide tactile feedback, try imagining a vertical pole as you peel your body away from the pole vertebrae by vertebrae and then uncurl your spine back up against the imaginary pole vertebrae by vertebrae.

Teaching points

- Maintain navel to spine throughout.

- Pay attention to your alignment.

- Keep your shoulders relaxed and down away from your ears.

- Ensure your weight is evenly distributed across your whole foot – think about the imaginary triangle at the bottom of each foot.

- Always start and end with the head. Be careful not to fling your head back as you return to an upright position.

Summing Up

All of the fundamentals are excellent preparation before you start the workout programme and some of the exercises can be used as a warm up before the main programme. Make sure that you practise the fundamentals and only move onto the main workout when you feel confident with all the fundamentals and Pilates principles.

Chapter Eight

The Exercises – Applying the Fundamentals

It is now time to apply everything you have learned so far to the main workout. Take your time and start with stage one of each exercise. There is no need to rush through, otherwise you will miss the vital point of Pilates. The golden rule of this method is quality not quantity if you are going to experience the full benefit of your Pilates practice. Do the movements in the order that they appear in the book, whether you do all 11 or fewer. If at anytime you need to refer back to the fundamentals then don't hesitate as this is how you will achieve the amazing results that you deserve.

The hundred

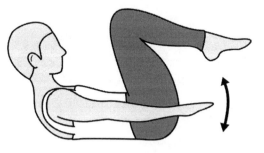

Aim

- To improve the skills needed for all the Pilates exercises, as these skills are important preparation for all Pilates movements.

- To strengthen your powerhouse – core stability muscles.

- To stimulate your circulatory system and warm up the body.

- To improve breathing and bring focus to your workout.

Stage one – how

- Lie on the mat in the starting position and check your alignment is correct.

- Navel to spine – as with all the exercises, avoid sucking in your stomach as this will cause you to hold your breath. Just imagine a heavy weight pressing down on your tummy. Take an in breath to prepare.

- On the out breath, navel to spine and bend one leg at a time to a table top position. When both legs are level, bring them together and gently squeeze your buttocks and thighs to help you maintain a stable and strong centre. (If this leg position causes you to strain then maintain the table top position but place the soles of your feet flat against a wall for extra support until you develop your core strength.)

- Maintaining navel to spine, lengthen forwards into an upper body curl (using the curl up fundamental principles). Bring your chin towards your chest and look towards your navel. Take an in breath and deepen navel to spine.

- Keep the tips of your shoulder blades in contact with the mat.

- Stretch your arms out with your palms facing down so they are hovering off the floor and with finger tips reaching across the room.

- On the out breath, pump your arms up and down for a count of five. On the in breath, pump your arms up and down for a count of five again.

- As you progress, you will repeat this cycle 10 times. To start with, do less, – such as two cycles – or the number of cycles that allows you to maintain the quality of the movement.

- End by lowering your head and torso and place the soles of your feet one at a time back onto the mat.

Stage two – progression

- Use the same set up and instructions as stage one.

- This time straighten your legs, keeping them together, up towards the ceiling. Maintain navel to spine and squeeze your buttocks and thighs.

Stage three

- As your abdominal strength improves, you will be able to lower your legs to a 45° angle or to the point just before your spine arches off the mat.

- Eventually your toes should be at eye level.

Visualisation

Imagine bouncing a tennis ball each side of your body, five times on the in breath and five times on the out breath for a cycle of 10.

Teaching points

- As with all the exercises, challenge yourself but do not strain. If you find stage one too strenuous then begin with keeping the soles of your feet flat on the mat.

- If you find your neck straining then rest your head back down to the mat.

- Only ever work within your range of movement to maintain the quality of the movement and to avoid injury. Then as you progress you can challenge yourself further.

- Work up to the total cycle of breaths but never exceed 10 breaths – five pumps for each out breath (exhale fully) and five pumps for each in breath for a total of 10 pumps. If you exceed this amount it will cause unnecessary stress on your system. If you find it difficult to keep count of the breaths, you could always make a recording on a dictaphone.

- The pumping motion should be short and vigorous, but at the same time the action should be smooth and tension free.

- Lengthen into the upper body curl position lifting your head, neck and spine as one unit. There should be no tension in your neck at any time.

- Do not arch your spine off the mat. Keep yourself firmly anchored to the mat, maintaining a level spine.

- Maintain navel to spine throughout the exercise and watch that your stomach doesn't pop up.

- Chin towards your chest.

- Keep your shoulders relaxed down in your back away from your ears, keeping your chest open.

Roll up

Aim

- To strengthen abdominal muscles.

- To develop spinal mobility and stability.

Stage one – how

- Sit tall on your seat bones, legs together, knees bent and feet flat on the mat.

- Place your hands behind your thighs, just below your knees.

- On the in breath, grow taller; imagine that piece of string drawing the crown of your head up towards the ceiling.

- On the out breath, navel to spine and curl your spine as much as possible with the top of your head towards your knees and create a 'C' curve in your spine as you roll it back towards the mat vertebrae by vertebrae.

- Stop when your arms are straight or, depending on your range of movement, stop before the arms straighten.

- On the in breath, round forward to the start maintaining the 'C' curve in your spine with your elbows bent and wide. Return to the start, restacking your spine vertebrae by vertebrae back up to an upright position. Navel to spine throughout.

- Repeat four to eight times.

Stage two – progression

- Increase your range of movement by letting your hands slide down your thighs and continue rolling back vertebrae by vertebrae until your spine lays flat on the mat. Keep your knees bent and feet flat on the mat at all times.

- Then maintaining navel to spine, roll back up vertebrae by vertebrae, reaching for your thighs towards your bent knees, keeping the 'C' curve in your spine throughout.

- Then, try to roll down and up with your hands long by your sides, palms face down.

Stage three

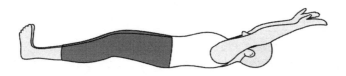

- Start by lying down flat along the mat in the supine position (on your back), with your arms straight behind your head without your ribcage flaring upwards (if necessary refer back to ribcage stability fundamental exercise).

- Legs extended along the mat and together, feet flexed with heels anchored to the mat.

- On the in breath, navel to spine and raise your arms above your head until your fingertips are reaching towards the ceiling.

- On the out breath, curl your head and shoulders off the mat until your head is between your arms.

- Continue to roll up vertebrae by vertebrae until your hands reach a point above your feet, maintaining the 'C' curve in your spine.

- On the in breath, maintain navel to spine and begin to reverse the movement vertebrae by vertebrae, rolling back until your shoulder blades reach the mat.

- On the out breath, finish by bringing your arms overhead and lower your head, returning to the start.

- Repeat three to five times.

Visualisation

Imagine holding onto a wooden broomstick handle and visualise someone holding onto the handle, pulling you upwards and forwards off the mat and then gently lowering you back down again.

Teaching points

- Only increase your range of movement when you are ready – and when mobility and strength allows.

- Keep your head aligned with your spine throughout.

- When lying on your back, do not allow your ribs to flare up as you take your arms overhead.

- Maintain navel to spine throughout.

- Do not allow your stomach to bulge.

- Keep your legs firmly anchored to the mat, pushing your heels away from your hips (feet flexed).

- Shoulders should be relaxed down, away from your ears.

- Chin towards your chest.

- Maintain the 'C' curve in your spine.

- Maintain a smooth rolling motion throughout with control.

Single leg circles

Aim

- To develop control and mobility in your hip joint.

- To work the abdominals.

Stage one – how

- Lie on the mat in the starting position and check your alignment is correct.

- Knees bent, feet flat on the mat, with your arms long down by your sides, palms down.

- Navel to spine and raise one leg to a table top position.

- On the out breath circle the raised knee across your body first, then down and around. On the in breath finish the circle as you bring your leg back to the start position. Start off with small circles and then gradually make the circles as big as your range of movement will allow.

■ Complete three to five repetitions. An out breath for the first half of the circle and an in breath as you complete the circle.

■ Then reverse the direction of the knee.

■ Repeat with your other leg.

Stage two – progression

■ Keep the same position on the mat as stage one.

■ Next as you bring your first leg to a table top position, try to straighten it up towards the ceiling and start the circles in both directions.

■ Repeat with your other leg.

Stage three

■ Keep the same position on the mat as stages one and two.

■ This time straighten your supporting leg along the mat and then straighten your working leg up towards the ceiling. You can either flex or point your feet.

■ Start circles in both directions and then repeat with your other leg.

Visualisation

Imagine your knee (stage one) or foot (stage two and three) is a pencil drawing circles on the ceiling – both anti-clockwise and clockwise.

Teaching points

■ Generate the movement from your hip.

■ Only increase the size of the circles if mobility will allow and stability can be maintained in the pelvis and ribcage.

- Maintain navel to spine throughout.

- Maintain a level pelvis and control over your hips throughout.

- Keep your neck, shoulders and chest relaxed, and maintain the length in the back of your neck.

Rolling like a ball

Aim

- To massage, stretch and reduce tension in your spine.

- To work the abdominals.

Stage one – how

- Sit on your seat bones and bend your knees towards your chest.

- Place both your hands around the your lower shins, but keep your knees slightly open while bringing your heels together and as close to your bottom as is comfortable.

- Navel to spine – lift both your feet off the mat, until you are balancing on your tailbone.

- Aim to round yourself into a ball shape by rounding your back, creating a 'C' curve and tucking your chin towards your chest. Keep your head aligned with the natural curve of your spine.
- Maintain this balanced position – eliminate the rolling motion at this stage.

Stage two – progression

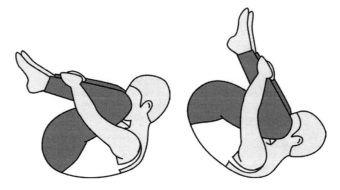

- Start in the same position as stage one in a balanced position at the front of the mat.
- On the in breath, navel to spine and using your abdominals initiate the rolling back like a ball onto your shoulder blades.
- On the out breath, maintaining navel to spine, roll back up to the start.
- Repeat four to six times.

Stage three

- Sit towards the front of the mat, bend your knees towards your chest and grab your ankles with your hands.
- Keep your heels together, bringing them closer towards your buttocks with the aim of achieving a more rounded and tighter shaped ball.
- On the in breath, navel to spine and roll back. On the out breath, return.
- Repeat four to six times.

Need2Know

Visualisation

Imagine your body as an inflated tyre rolling back and forth in touch with the ground.

Teaching points

- Maintain navel to spine throughout.

- Feel each vertebrae in your spine roll into the mat and return vertebrae by vertebrae.

- Maintain the 'C' curve in your spine throughout, keeping your head in alignment with the natural curve of your spine.

- Keep your shoulders down in your back away from your ears and keep them open rather than forward towards your chest.

- Don't roll back too far as this will place stress on your neck. Stop at the bottom of your shoulder blades.

- Work from your abdominals not your shoulders.

- Ensure you have a safe amount of space behind you as you roll back.

Single leg stretch

Aim

- To develop co-ordination skills and stability of movement.

- To work the abdominals.

Stage one – how

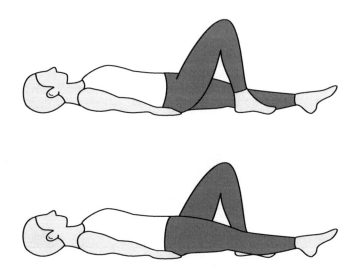

- Lie on the mat in the starting position and check your alignment is correct.

- Knees bent and feet flat on the mat with both legs and feet hip width apart.

- Start with a few simple leg slides to help develop co-ordination skills and correct engagement of core stability muscles. Take an in breath to prepare.

- On the out breath, navel to spine and lengthen one leg away along the mat until your leg is flat against the mat. Keep your knees soft.

- On the in breath, maintaining navel to spine, slide the same leg back towards your buttocks to return to the start position.

- Alternate from left to right leg.

Stage two – progression

- Lie on the mat and check your alignment is correct. This time bring both knees in towards your chest. Take an in breath to prepare.

- On the out breath, navel to spine and lift your upper body into an upper body curl (you can always lower your head back down to the mat if you are straining).

- Grasp your right ankle with your right hand and grasp your right knee with your left hand.

- Navel to spine and extend your left leg to the ceiling to a 90° angle.

- On the in breath, maintaining navel to spine, switch legs and hand position simultaneously, keeping your elbows out from your body and raised.

- On the out breath, switch again.

- Repeat three times.

Stage three

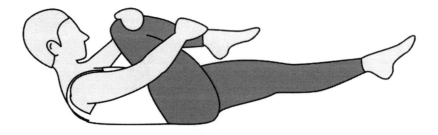

- Same positions as stage two with upper body curl, knees bent into chest and apply the same hand positions. Take an in breath to prepare.

- On the out breath, navel to spine and straighten one leg away at a lowered height, at an angle just high enough to keep your back from arching off the mat, avoiding lowering your extended leg below hip level.

- On the in breath, maintaining navel to spine, change legs and hand positions simultaneously.

- On the out breath, switch again.

- Repeat five to eight times.

Visualisation

Imagine a glass of water balancing on your lower tummy.

Teaching points

- Maintain navel to spine throughout.

- Keep your torso still throughout.

- Your extended leg must stay off the mat, maintaining level hips.

- The breathing pattern could change to 'out breath' for two leg stretches and 'in breath' for two leg stretches. This may help you to create more rhythm.

- Keep shoulders relaxed and down away from your ears.

- Chin towards your chest.
- Do not arch your spine off the mat, keep yourself firmly anchored to the mat, maintaining a level spine.
- Don't allow your stomach to bulge.
- Stretch out from your hip.

Double leg stretch

Aim

- To develop stability in your torso.
- To strengthen abdominals.
- To develop co-ordination skills and flow.

Stage one – how

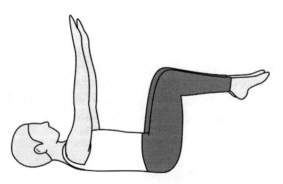

- Lie on the mat in the starting position and check your alignment is correct. Take an in breath to prepare.
- On the out breath, navel to spine and lift one leg at a time to a table top position and place your right hand on your right knee and your left hand on your left knee.

- On the in breath, stretch your arms up straight, towards the ceiling.

- On the out breath, maintaining navel to spine, sweep your arms out to the sides and reach round to grasp your knees in the starting position.

- Hold position and circle arms five more times.

Stage two – progression

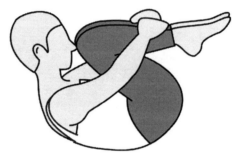

- Lie on the mat with your knees bent towards your chest and your hands on your shins. Take an in breath to prepare.

- On the out breath, navel to spine and lift into an upper body curl (or if you find that you are straining then keep your head on the mat).

- On the in breath, maintaining navel to spine, simultaneously stretch your body long by moving your arms overhead and straightening your legs towards the ceiling at a 90° angle. If your head is on the mat then it's important to maintain this angle to prevent strain to your neck and lower back.

- On the out breath, maintaining navel to spine, simultaneously circle your arms around from overhead and out to the sides, drawing your knees back in towards your chest.

- Repeat five times – using the in breath to stretch and the out breath to return to starting position.

Stage three

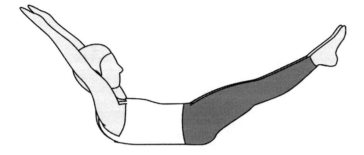

- Same instruction as stage two. As your abdominal strength increases, lower the angle of your legs to just above eye level at about a 45° angle, remaining in the upper body curl position.

- Squeeze your buttocks and upper thighs tightly together as you extend your legs to give support to your lower back.

Visualisation

Imagine the trunk of your body being cemented to the ground as you stretch your arms and legs out and back to the centre.

Teaching points

- Navel to spine throughout.

- Don't allow your ribs to flare up or your stomach to bulge.

- Don't allow your back to arch off the mat – imprint your lower back into the mat throughout.

- Chin towards your chest.

- Keep your toes pointed and feet and legs together.

- In stage three, maintain an upper body curled up position. Don't allow your shoulders to drop and keep them relaxed down away from your ears.

Spine stretch

Aim

- To develop spinal articulation.
- To work the abdominals and promote deep Pilates breathing.
- To enhance good posture and stretch your hamstrings.

Stage one – how

- Sit up tall onto your seat bones on the mat (if this is difficult then place a folded towel underneath you to help you sit up tall).
- Extend your legs along the mat in front of you, keeping them a little more than shoulder width apart. Bend your knees slightly if you have tight hamstrings.

- Toes flexed towards the ceiling and lengthen your arms out in front of you at shoulder height, parallel to the mat. Keep palms facing down.

- On the in breath, navel to spine and lengthen the trunk of your body upwards, imagining a piece of string pulling the crown of your head up towards the ceiling.

- On the out breath, maintain navel to spine and roll down and forwards starting with your chin towards your chest creating a 'C' curve shape in your spine vertebrae by vertebrae. Stretch your arms forwards as far as your range of movement will allow.

- On the in breath, reverse the motion as you restack your spine back to the start.

- Repeat three to five times.

Stage two – progression

- Same instructions as stage one. As you become more limber you can then go from having your knees slightly bent to keeping them straight, a little more than shoulder width apart, keeping your feet flexed up towards the ceiling.

- Gradually increase your range of movement by reaching further forward and curl your spine even deeper.

Stage three

- Same instructions as stage two. Now try to increase your range of movement even more, keeping your feet flexed and pushing through your heels to increase the stretch in your calves, hamstrings and spine.

Visualisation

Think of creating a 'C' curve shape in your spine as if rolling over a beach ball.

Teaching points

- Navel to spine throughout.

- Keep your shoulders relaxed and down away from your ears.

- Exhale all the air from your lungs as you stretch forwards.

- Don't slump, collapsing onto your lungs.

- Maintain length in the back of your neck and as you curl forwards bringing your chin towards your chest.

- Keep your feet flexed and knees facing up towards the ceiling to avoid them rolling in or outwards.

- Don't force the movement. Your range of movement will increase as you develop more flexibility.

- As you roll back up to the start, avoid rolling backwards.

The saw

Aim

- To stretch your hamstrings.

- To work your waistline.

- To develop spinal rotation.

Stage one – how

Need2Know

- Sit up tall onto your seat bones.

- Extend your legs along the mat in front of you keeping them a little more than shoulder width apart. Bend your knees slightly if you have tight hamstrings.

- Toes should be flexed up towards the ceiling. Arms straight out to the side in a 'T' shape, and palms face down.

- On the in breath, navel to spine and lengthen the trunk of your body upwards, imagining a piece of string pulling the crown of your head up towards the ceiling.

- On the out breath, maintain navel to spine and rotate from your waist to one side.

- On the in breath, return to a tall position back to the centre.

- On the out breath, rotate from the waist to your other side.

- On the in breath, return back to the centre again.

- Practise this rotational movement three times each side to help prepare you for the next progression.

Stage two – progression

- Same position as stage one, but if flexibility will allow, go from having slightly bent knees to straightening your legs along the mat a little more than shoulder width apart. Keep your feet flexed up towards the ceiling.

- On the in breath, navel to spine and lengthen the trunk of your body upwards, imagining a piece of string pulling the crown of your head up towards the ceiling.

- On the out breath, maintain navel to spine and rotate your body from the waist to one side and reach forwards folding over your leg as if sawing off your little toe with the edge of your hand. Reach your other arm back behind you raising it as high as your range of movement allows. Keep your seat bones firmly anchored to the mat.

- On the in breath, rotate back up to the centre and on the out breath repeat on the other side.

- Repeat three to five times each side.

Stage three

- Same instruction as stage two. Now try to increase your range of movement even more. Keep your feet flexed up towards the ceiling, pushing through your heels to increase the stretch in your calves, hamstrings and spine.

Visualisation

Think of wringing water from a flannel. So as you rotate your body forwards, think of wringing out every last bit of air from your lungs by exhaling fully.

Teaching points

- Maintain navel to spine throughout.

- Keep your heels and seat bones anchored to the floor. Imagine you have two £50 notes under your seat bones and you don't want them to blow away. Stretch out through your heels.

- As you return to the centre, lengthen the trunk of your body upwards. Think of that piece of string pulling the crown of your head up towards the ceiling. Don't arch your back.

- As you reach forwards, think about lengthening through the crown of your head.

- Keep your shoulders relaxed and down away from your ears.

- Keep your feet flexed and knees facing the ceiling to avoid rolling in or outwards.

- Initiate the rotation from the waist and exhale all the air from your lungs as you reach forward.

- Don't force the movement. Your range of motion will increase as you develop more flexibility.

- Don't slump, collapsing onto your lungs.

The swan

You should seek medical advice if you have any back problems before attempting this exercise.

Aim

- To strengthen and stretch your back, neck and shoulder muscles.

- To counteract the forward flexion position that we habitually do throughout the day.

Stage one – how

- Lie on your front with your forehead resting on the mat. Place your palms flat on the mat directly under your shoulders. Bring your legs and feet together stretching them out behind you.

- On the in breath, navel to spine and begin straightening your arms up, palms pressing down onto the mat. Only lift within your range of movement. Don't drop your head back; keep your neck long and in alignment with your spine.

- Continue to inhale, maintaining navel to spine until you have reached your full range of movement without strain in your lower back, shoulders or neck.

- On the out breath, maintain navel to spine as you bend your arms, lowering your pelvis, abdomen, ribcage, chest and finally your head back down to the start.

- Repeat three to five times.

- As with all the exercises, stay with the modification until you are ready both physically and mentally to progress. Then you can use this stage to warm up your back muscles before the swan dive progressions.

Stage two – progression

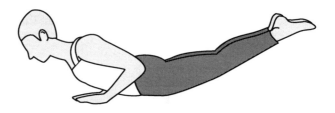

- Lie on your tummy in the same position as stage one.

- On the in breath, navel to spine and begin straightening your arms, palms down on the mat. Lift as far as your range of movement will allow. Don't drop your head back. Keep your neck long and in alignment with your spine.

- Continue to inhale, maintaining navel to spine until you have reached your full range of movement without strain in your lower back, shoulders and neck. Stretch your legs and feet out further behind you.

- On the out breath, maintain navel to spine and bend your arms, keeping palms flat against the mat as you rock forwards onto your ribcage and upper chest, with your legs stretching out away from you hovering off the floor. Keep them together and straight.

- On the in breath, push your palms down into the mat to help push you up again. Your legs will return back down to the mat.

- Repeat three to five times and then drop back into the rest position to release.

Stage three

- Same instructions as stage two. This time on the out breath release your arms as you rock forwards onto your ribcage and upper chest. Reach your arms – palms facing one another – straight out in front of you beyond your head and in line with your ears and stretch your legs back up towards the ceiling.

- On the in breath, maintaining navel to spine and the arc shape of your body, rock back, rising up on your pelvis and lift your head, chest and arms – imagine throwing a beach ball behind you over your head.

- On the out breath, rock forwards again onto your ribcage and upper chest, still holding the arc shape of your body.

- Rock back and fourth three to five times.

Visualisation

Imagine your body in a fully inflated tyre, rolling back and fourth.

Teaching points

- Maintain navel to spine throughout.
- Squeeze your buttocks together to support your lower back.
- Relax your shoulders down and away from your ears.
- Don't throw your head back. Lengthen the back of your neck by lifting from your chest.
- Legs and feet should be together stretching out behind you.
- Maintain the arc shape of your body.
- As with all the exercises, maintain awareness of how your body feels and stop if you feel any strain or pain.
- As you lift up in the movement, think about stretching forwards and up vertebrae by vertebrae.

The side kick series

Aim

- To stretch tight hip flexors (the group of muscles that flex the hip bringing the thigh and the trunk of the body closer together) and hamstrings.
- To work your buttocks, hips and abdominals.
- To improve stability and balance.

Need2Know

Stage one – how

- Lie on your side and rest you head on your arm which should be extended straight, in line with your spine. Place your other hand on the mat in front of your chest.

- Lengthen your legs along the mat and stack your shoulders, hips, knees and ankles. Bend at the hip so that your legs are at a slight forward angle to your body.

- Bend your leg nearest to the mat and move it slightly forward to help stabilise your torso and press your bent leg into the mat. Take an in breath to prepare.

- On the out breath, navel to spine and lift your top leg hip level.

- On the in breath, maintain navel to spine with your toes softly pointed, kick your lengthened top leg forwards working within your range of movement and pulse twice – two small kicks. If you're struggling to maintain balance you can bend your top leg as you swing it back and forth.

- On the out breath, maintain navel to spine and swing your top leg back behind you in a straight line and pulse twice.

- Repeat three to five times. Then turn over and repeat on your other side.

If you can maintain your balance, attempt to rest your top arm along the top of your thigh. You can also straighten your bottom leg along the mat directly under your top leg – hip over hip and anchor your whole body to the mat.

Stage two – progression

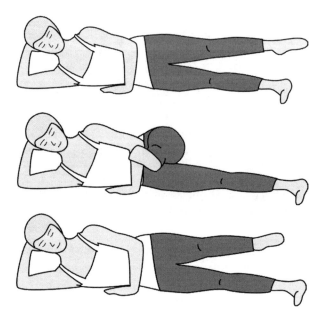

- Same instructions as stage one. If you haven't attempted to already, straighten your bottom leg along the mat directly under your top leg, still maintaining a slight forward angle to your body.

- Come up onto your elbow and rest your head on your hand, keep your elbow in line with your tailbone. Your top hand should rest on the mat in front of your chest or if balance can be maintained rest your top arm along the top of your thigh.

- On the in breath, maintain navel to spine and kick your lengthened top leg forward and pulse twice.

- On the out breath, kick the same leg back and pulse twice.

- Repeat three to five times. Then turn over and repeat on your other side.

Stage three

- Same instructions as stage two. This time, your top hand, which you were using for stability by placing it on the floor, should now be placed behind your head. Keep your elbow lifted and back to open up through your chest and maintain the line of your body.

- On the in breath, maintain navel to spine and kick your lengthened top leg forward and pulse twice.

- On the out breath, kick the same leg back and pulse twice.

- Repeat three to five times. Then turn over to repeat on your other side. The change in hand position will further change your stability as it is no longer resting on the mat providing you with support. You will really need to engage your core stability muscles (navel to spine) to maintain balance.

Visualisation

To maintain a strong, firm centre with stability, imagine two panes of glass both sides of your torso. You want to avoid falling against them.

Teaching points

- Maintain navel to spine throughout.

- Don't collapse through your waist and try to maintain a strong, firm centre.

- To begin with, keep your range of movement small as you kick your top leg forward and back to avoid losing your balance. Increase your range of movement as you progress and are able to maintain stability.

- Keep your shoulders, hips, knees and ankles stacked in alignment and maintain long length throughout your body without allowing your chest and shoulders to collapse forwards.

- Don't arch your back and thrust your ribs forward as you kick your top leg back.

The side kick lift

How

- Remain in side kick position on the mat – choose the appropriate positioning of your hands as described in side kick stages one, two and three, depending on your current level.

- Rotate your foot and leg in your hip joint and stretch out of your hip.

- Navel to spine and on the in breath kick your top leg high up towards the ceiling with toes softly pointed.

- On the out breath, maintaining navel to spine and flex your foot and lower your leg back down to the start.

- Repeat five to 10 times and then turn over and repeat on the other side. You can do both the side kick and the side kick lift on one side before you change to the other side.

Visualisation

As you lower your leg, imagine someone tugging at your heel to promote lengthening through the heel.

Teaching points

■ Maintain navel to spine throughout.

■ Work within your range of movement until stability and mobility increases.

■ Avoid allowing your top hip to roll backwards as you rotate your leg and foot in your hip joint.

■ Keep your shoulders, hips, knees and ankles stacked in alignment and maintain long length throughout your body without allowing your chest and shoulders to collapse forwards.

The seal

Aim

■ To massage your spine and improve hip joint flexibility.

■ To work abdominals.

■ To improve balance and co-ordination.

Stage one – how

■ Sit at the front of the mat. Bend your knees out to the sides so that you bring your heels together.

- Create a 'C' curve shape in your spine, and tuck your chin towards your chest.

- Slide your hands in between your legs and bring them to the outside of your ankles, cupping them around your feet and pressing the soles of your feet together.

- Navel to spine and come onto your tailbone by lifting your heels slightly off the mat. Practise balancing in this position.

Stage two – progression

- Same position as stage one. In the balanced position, as you take an in breath, maintaining navel to spine, roll back vertebrae by vertebrae onto your shoulder blades.

- On the out breath, maintaining navel to spine, roll back up to the start vertebrae by vertebrae to the balanced position.

- Repeat four to six times.

Stage three

- Same instructions as stage two. In the balance position as you take an in breath, maintain navel to spine and roll back vertebrae by vertebrae onto your shoulder blades with your feet just over your head.

- Maintain navel to spine and balance in this position. Part your feet and then bring them back together to clap them together three times.

- On the out breath, roll back up vertebrae by vertebrae to the balance position and again part your feet and then bring them back together to clap them three times.

- Repeat four to six times.

If, as you roll on to your back, you find it difficult to master the clapping action with your feet then leave it out and only do the clapping action in the forward balanced position.

Visualisation

Imagine you are a rocking horse, rocking back and fourth.

Teaching points

- Maintain navel to spine throughout.

- Use control not momentum, though keep the motion smooth.

- Maintain a 'C' curve shape in your spine and keep your neck in alignment with your spine. Chin towards your chest.

- Relax your shoulders down and away from your ears.

- Feel each vertebrae in your spine roll into the mat and then return vertebrae by vertebrae.

- Ensure you have a safe amount of space behind you as you roll back.

Summing Up

Now you have all the instructions you need to perform a safe and very effective workout. Work through stage one first and when you feel ready, work through stage two. As you become fitter, you will be ready to attempt the stage three progressions.

Although it's good to challenge yourself, ensure that you stay at all times within your range of movement, even if that means never attempting the other stages. Read and pay attention to all the teaching points as this will be an essential guide for helping you to achieve effective results safely. Most importantly, enjoy your workout!

Chapter Nine

What Next?

Private, group or go it alone?

Classes can be held in private studios, village halls, leisure centres or even in your own home. Sessions can involve the matwork alone or some studios also use equipment. It is a good idea to have the help and guidance of a trained Pilates instructor as their expert eye will pick up on any incorrect body alignments and they will ensure that you perform the movements correctly. If you follow the instructions in this book carefully, you will be able to achieve a safe, healthy and effective Pilates workout at home. Although, once you get bitten by the Pilates bug, you will find yourself hungry for more information and there are many fantastic instructors and lots of great books and DVDs available to you.

Private sessions

There is no question about it – having a one on one session with a highly qualified instructor is a very effective way of helping you to understand your body and how you can reach your personal fitness goals and needs. Having the full attention of an instructor will ensure that you are performing the movements in a precise way as intended. Your alignment will be under continual observation and corrected as required as you perform the movements. Private sessions are more expensive but they are a worthwhile investment if you can afford them. Even just having a few one to one sessions will be very beneficial to you before joining a group. This way the instructor can assess your body and movement patterns and help you better understand the exercises as you perform them, giving you a head start.

'If you follow the instructions in this book carefully, you will be able to achieve a safe, healthy and effective Pilates workout at home.'

You could also choose to have a session once a month as this will provide you with regular feedback, as well as giving you a chance to ask anything that you are unsure about. Another option is to share a session with two or three others to help keep the costs down.

Group sessions

It is wise to avoid a group session where there are a large number of participants in a class, especially if you are a beginner. As you can imagine, if there are large numbers in one class, then it is very hard for an instructor, no matter how good they are, to keep a watchful eye on everyone. Pilates is a very precise method, so if you perform a movement incorrectly, you will lose the vital benefits of the movement at best and at worse risk an injury. Therefore, always aim to attend a group matwork class with no more than 12 other participants in one session – and less is even better.

Choosing the right instructor

You should always seek a highly qualified instructor. Perhaps by answering the following questions you can choose wisely, as a teacher can make or break the Pilates experience.

- Do you have a good rapport with your instructor and are they approachable as well as motivating and inspiring?
- Does your instructor provide regular feedback and effective guidance throughout a session?
- Are they confident in the full repertoire of all the Pilates exercises?
- Does the instructor keep up to date with their knowledge and seek continual education?
- Are they able to verify completion of their Pilates training and have they trained at a reputable centre that maintains high standards?
- Can they demonstrate a strong background in Pilates history and philosophy, as well as having knowledgeable understanding of the basic human anatomy?

- Do they behave professionally at all times?

Remember, you may or may not be lucky enough to find a suitable instructor straightaway. Therefore, never be afraid to change instructors as everyone teaches differently and some will suit your needs better than others.

Preparing for your first class

The guidelines earlier on in the 'before you begin' section apply to any Pilates session, whether at home or in a class. As well as for comfort, choose clothes that show off your body shape clearly. This will make it easier for an instructor to pick up on incorrect alignment and practice. Water may not always be available on the premises, so it might be wise to take your own. Also, check with the instructor whether they supply the mats or if you need to bring your own, as well as any other requirements. If you use your own mat, ensure that it is padded enough to protect your spine.

It is important to let your instructor know of any medical conditions you have and to check with your GP before you take part in any form of exercise. Your instructor is very likely to ask you to fill out a health questionnaire for your own safety as well as providing them with other important information. This information will provide your instructor with your health and fitness goals and they can then ensure a realistic, safe and progressive programme of the Pilates method.

Motivation – stick with it!

Trust the Pilates method – it works! There is no magic wand for instant results, but you will feel great after your first session and in time you will see amazing results too. Once you really understand the method, you will find yourself looking forward to your next Pilates session which is why it's so important to incorporate all the Pilates principles into your practice. This is when you will truly experience the magic and art of Pilates!

'There is no magic wand for instant results, but you will feel great after your first session and in time you will see amazing results too.'

Another way to stay motivated is to invest in some nice workout clothes that not only feel comfortable but look good too. They don't have to be expensive, but if you feel good then you will have a far more positive association when you workout. This will enhance your sense of wellbeing, encouraging you to want to keep going and make your workout part of your life.

Regular practise

It is very important to establish a regular routine of Pilates. Ideally, if you can, practise on a daily basis even if for a short time. As time goes on, you will find yourself extending your sessions the more you feel the benefits. The main point being that the more you put into practising, the more you will gain – not just in a session but across your whole life too. The physical and mental conditioning that Pilates gives you will provide you with an excellent platform in life.

Summing Up

The magic of Pilates can be missed if you do not seek out the right instructor and situation that works for you. If you are not feeling and seeing the benefits of Pilates then the chances are that you are not approaching it in the right way and perhaps have not found the right teacher.

By following the advice laid out in this chapter, you stand a great chance of being one of the many people whose health and wellbeing have significantly improved by the practice of the true Pilates method.

Chapter Ten

Applying Pilates to Everyday Life

Day-to-day Pilates

Pilates retrains the body and mind, and bad habits are highlighted and corrected. All the skills and benefits gained from your Pilates practice will become automatic in both movement and at rest, and can be applied to everyday activities, not just when you workout at home or in a studio.

Pilates and stress

Due to the concentration required to perform the Pilates movements correctly while incorporating all the Pilates principles, over time the exercises themselves become almost meditative. Stress levels will be reduced as you release tension held in the body. After a full workout you will feel refreshed, energised and in tune with your body.

'I have a very stressful and demanding job and need to deliver results. Pilates truly gives me time back which allows me to clear my head. The mental focus needed as I perform the movements gives me very little time to think of other things that have happened during the day. After a Pilates session I feel more mentally focused and calm, making me far more effective in all that I do, including coping with my job's demands.'

Philip, Channel account manager.

'All the skills and benefits gained from your Pilates practice will become automatic in both movement and at rest, and can be applied to everyday activities, not just when you workout at home or in a studio.'

Pilates for the older adult

Pilates provides a safe, gentle and very effective workout for the older adult. Over the years, bad habits, along with the aging body, can cause deterioration in a person's daily function. Bad posture can set in and the body becomes tight and inflexible. Muscle strength declines and bone density needs to be addressed to prevent the onset of problems such as osteoporosis. The importance of resistance exercises used in Pilates can really help older people improve their strength and bone density.

'The control and core strength that is developed in Pilates will enable better control over everyday movements, leading to improved balance too.'

The control and core strength that is developed in Pilates will enable better control over everyday movements, leading to improved balance too. Studies also show that the pelvic floor and deep abdominal muscles work together to help keep the lower back healthy and to prevent urinary leakage, which can be common in older adults. Therefore, all these factors can be addressed using Pilates in a safe way, making it a great workout for the older adult.

'I was always interested in keeping fit, but it wasn't until I retired that I wanted to do all I could to keep my aging body healthy. It was more about feeling good rather than looking good at that point in my life. I also wanted to prolong my independence for as long as possible. I enjoy playing with my grandchildren and didn't want that to end anytime soon. Even the simple things in life that we take for granted, like getting up out of a chair without a struggle, became important as I got older. I knew I would have to look after my bones and muscles for strength and balance. So when I took up Pilates, I found the low impact exercises really improved my flexibility and strength. I felt better than I had done in years! After all, it was my body and I was the only one who could make my life better. I never realised how amazing our bodies are and I have even got my grandchildren involved in learning that very fact.'

Gerry Kent, retired teacher.

Pilates and back problems

There are many reasons why people suffer with back pain and it is impossible for an instructor to prescribe a remedial exercise programme without a proper diagnosis. Medical advice must be sought first before attempting any exercise programme; otherwise you may risk further damage. Having said that, the majority of back problems are caused by poor posture habits, poor movement patterns and muscle imbalances, which makes Pilates an ideal choice in helping with these cases. Pilates is also a great preventive measure in helping people to avoid possible back problems later on in life.

> 'Thanks to Pilates, I have strengthened my core stability muscles and therefore lessoned my back pain considerably. Much more fun than going to the chiropractor!'
>
> Maggie, housewife.

Pilates and sport

Pilates is very effective for those who want to improve their performance in all types of sports. As core abdominal strength is developed, there is then greater control and balance over the movements required for your sport. Arms and legs can then work from a strong and stable centre at optimum function. For instance, nothing is as impressive as an athlete or figure skater who has complete control over their body and can make the movements look effortless.

The development of concentration needed in Pilates enables you to bring mental focus to your sport. Precision is another positive side effect of Pilates as you learn economy of every single movement which is a valuable skill as energy levels and time is never wasted – a crucial skill needed in many sports.

The correct use of the breath allows the body to operate at its optimum level, as well as providing a vehicle for concentration and calm when under pressure, which can be especially true in competitive sports. You will also develop muscle balance in Pilates too; again this will enable your body to work at its very best. Flow, another Pilates principle, enables correct muscle recruitment at the right time. For example, if two people are doing the exact same movement, the comparison between the two can look very different. This is due to flow in one person and the lack of it in the other person.

'Through Pilates, my abdominal strength has improved. I have the strength through my centre as I stretch up to take a serve, making it far more powerful and effective. My performance has improved significantly.'

Jake, tennis player and university student.

Summing Up

Pilates can help you in all that you do – whether it is for health, sport or everyday life in general. It is wise to establish with an instructor what you want to get out of your Pilates practice so that they can help you to achieve your goals. However, whatever your reasons, you will always get more benefits beyond your personal goals from regular workouts as you condition both your body and mind. You will feel and look fantastic!

Help List

About.com Guide to Pilates

www.pilates.about.com
Free information resource for Pilates covering a number of Pilates related topics.

Classical Pilates

www.classicalpilates.net
Provides contact details of traditionally trained Pilates teachers worldwide. The classical Pilates method's goal is to preserve Joseph Pilates' traditional method of mental and physical conditioning through teaching, continuing education and instructional materials.

Easy Vigour

www.easyvigour.net.nz
Free information resource for Pilates mat work and therapeutic exercises.

Pilates Foundation

www.pilatesfoundation.com
A not-for-profit organisation, the Pilates Foundation is committed to establishing and maintaining certification, and continuing education standards at the very highest level.

Pilates Method Alliance (PMA)

www.pilatesmethodalliance.org
The Pilates Method Alliance® (PMA®) is the international, not-for-profit, professional association dedicated to the teachings of Joseph and Clara Pilates. Establishing certification and continuing education standards, and promoting the Pilates method of exercise.

Pilates.uk

www.pilates.co.uk
An online Pilates reference source providing lots of information and links dedicated to the Pilates method of exercise.

Book List

The Anatomy of Pilates
By Paul Massey, Lotus Publishing, Chichester, 2009.

The Everything Pilates Book
By Amy Taylor Alpers and Rachel Taylor Segal, Adams Media, USA, 2002.

Pilates
By Rael Isacowitz, Human Kinetics, USA, 2006.

The Pilates Body
By Brooke Siler, Michael Joseph, Broadway, 2000.

The Pilates Method of Physical and Mental Conditioning
By Philip Friedman and Gail Eisen, Penguin, London, 2005.

Pilates' Return to Life Through Contrology
By Joseph Pilates and William John Miller, Presentation Dynamics, USA, 1998.

Your Health
By Joseph Pilates, Presentation Dynamics, USA, 1998.

Need - 2 - Know

Available Titles Include ...

Allergies A Parent's Guide
ISBN 978-1-86144-064-8 £8.99

Autism A Parent's Guide
ISBN 978-1-86144-069-3 £8.99

Drugs A Parent's Guide
ISBN 978-1-86144-043-3 £8.99

Dyslexia and Other Learning Difficulties
A Parent's Guide   ISBN 978-1-86144-042-6 £8.99

Bullying A Parent's Guide
ISBN 978-1-86144-044-0 £8.99

Epilepsy The Essential Guide
ISBN 978-1-86144-063-1 £8.99

Teenage Pregnancy The Essential Guide
ISBN 978-1-86144-046-4 £8.99

Gap Years The Essential Guide
ISBN 978-1-86144-079-2 £8.99

How to Pass Exams A Parent's Guide
ISBN 978-1-86144-047-1 £8.99

Child Obesity A Parent's Guide
ISBN 978-1-86144-049-5 £8.99

Applying to University The Essential Guide
ISBN 978-1-86144-052-5 £8.99

ADHD The Essential Guide
ISBN 978-1-86144-060-0 £8.99

Student Cookbook - Healthy Eating The Essential Guide
ISBN 978-1-86144-061-7 £8.99

Stress The Essential Guide
ISBN 978-1-86144-054-9 £8.99

Adoption and Fostering A Parent's Guide
ISBN 978-1-86144-056-3 £8.99

Special Educational Needs A Parent's Guide
ISBN 978-1-86144-057-0 £8.99

The Pill An Essential Guide
ISBN 978-1-86144-058-7 £8.99

University A Survival Guide
ISBN 978-1-86144-072-3 £8.99

Diabetes The Essential Guide
ISBN 978-1-86144-059-4 £8.99

View the full range at **www.need2knowbooks.co.uk**. To order our titles, call **01733 898103**, email **sales@n2kbooks.com** or visit the website.

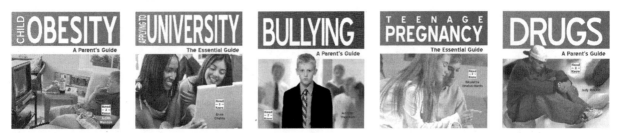

Need - 2 - Know, Remus House, Coltsfoot Drive, Peterborough, PE2 9JX